TEEN CHOICES

How to Make Better Decisions

Larry Shirer
2021

Author: Larry Shirer

Title: **TEEN CHOICES:**
HOW TO MAKE BETTER DECISIONS

Subjects: Dealing With Life Shaping Decisions; Decision Making Process &Techniques; Values and Principles for Living; Worldview; Search for Meaning.

ISBN: 9781667825120
Ebook ISBN: 9781667825137

Printed in USA

First Edition 2021

Author Web Site: larryspointstoponder.com

Cover photo by Ethan Johnson on Unsplash

TEEN CHOICES

TABLE OF CONTENTS

E. Practice Compassion.

F. Be Generous.

G. Be Grateful.

H. Accept Responsibility.

I. Maintain Self-Control.

J. Seek and Preserve Beauty.

K. Seek Balance and Harmony.

L. Demonstrate Respect and Reverence for Nature.

M. Use Time Wisely.

N. Live Every Day.

O. Relish Experiences.

P. Practice Mindfulness.

Q. Select a Vocation.

R. Face Up to Adversity

A. These Substances Kill People.

B. Health Effects.

C. Behavior Modification.

D. Distorted Self Perception.

E. Addiction.

F. Effects on Others.

G. Peer Pressure.

A. Process Criteria.

B. Process Outline.

1. Frame the Issue.

2. Identify and Gather Relevant Information.

3. Identify and Clearly Define Alternatives.

4. Consider the Likely Consequences.

5. Consider the Impact on Others.

6. Test the Possible Choices Against Your Values.

7. Test the Possible Choices Against Your Goals

and Objectives.
8. Tune into Your Intuition.
9. Think It Through.
10. Make a Decision.
11. Implement It.
12. Evaluate Past Decisions.

A. Brainstorming.
B. Lateral Thinking.
C. Scamper.
D. Pros & Cons.
E. Matrix Analysis.
F. Probabilities and Expected Values.

A. Spirituality and Religion.
B. Purpose.
C. Meaning.
D. Wisdom.
E. Love.

A. Sharpen Your Decision Making Skills.
1. Recognize the Importance of Decision Making.
2. Seek Knowledge, Truth and Wisdom.
3. Develop and Apply a Process.
4. Evaluate the Importance of Your Decisions.
5. Carefully Consider the Context.
6. Develop Your "Systems Thinking" Abilities.
7. View the Situation from the Other Person's
   Perspective.
8. Think It Through.

B. Follow Your Conscience.
   1. Act Morally and Ethically.
   2. Seek and Tell the Truth, Always.
   3. Care About People.
   4. Practice Personal Integrity.
   5. Accept Responsibility.
   6. Meet Commitments.
   7. Respect and Preserve Our Natural World.

C. Sharpen Your Personal Skills.
   1. Learn to Learn.
   2. Learn to Listen.
   3. Read.
   4. Use Time Wisely.
   5. Control What You Say When You Talk to Yourself.
   6. Think Before You Speak.
   7. Be Adaptive.
   8. Be Persistent.

D. Appreciate Life.
   1. Choose to Think.
   2. Choose to Make Your Life Meaningful.
   3. Choose to Let Your Life Speak.
   4. Choose to Really Live.

TEEN CHOICES
HOW TO MAKE BETTER DECISIONS

PART I

THINKING ABOUT DECISION MAKING

The teen years are tough! They are the time when youth are formed as persons. Young people are forced to deal with many choices. Some are difficult and have long term implications. Thinking about decision making, developing relevant skills and preparing yourself for making effective choices can help improve the results of your decisions.

A. PURPOSE

The purpose of this book is to encourage you to think about decision making and to help you:

- *understand and appreciate what a significant role decision making plays in your life.*
- *develop an effective process for improving the quality of your decisions.*
- *think through and select the assumptions and context within which you make decisions.*
- *understand some of the relevant concerns and considerations that impact the quality of choices.*
- *Identify and effectively deal with some life shaping decisions.*
- *appreciate how making better decisions can improve the quality of your life.*
- *make better decisions!*

B. THE IMPORTANCE AND SCOPE OF DECISION MAKING

Choices matter! Individual decisions, the choices we make, literally determine the course and quality of our lives. Who we are, what we do, our mental and emotional state, who and what we will become, all depend largely upon the <u>decisions</u> we make. Our happiness, success, health, achievements, morality and the extent to which our lives have meaning are determined primarily by the quality of our decisions. Aristotle, a respected Greek philosopher, observed long ago that "we become what we are as persons by the decisions that we make." That truth hasn't changed. The quality of our lives is determined by the decisions we make.

We make lots of decisions. The only thing we do more than make decisions is breathe. We make hundreds of decisions every day. Many are not earth shaking – what should I wear today? Which cereal should I have for breakfast? Some are life-changing - What career should I pursue? Should I go into debt to attend college? Is she/he the right spouse for me? Should I "try" addictive substances? Unfortunately, other than perhaps "fretting" a little more, we often approach important decisions much like we do minor decisions.

Decisions drive everything. Decisions determine whether our nation goes to war and sends our young people off to fight and die. Decisions determine whether our economy grows or stagnates. Decisions determine whether our planet can continue to support life as we know it. Our fate is determined by our personal decisions, by the decisions of elected officials, bureaucrats, corporate executives and others in positions of influence. The choices we make when we vote at the ballot box and when we express our opinions, with our voices, with our feet and with our spending money, all matter. The future of our economy, our country, and our planet will be determined by the quality of individual and collective human decisions.

We have access to huge amounts of information and many options. We are required to choose: values, goals and objectives, careers, where to reside, a spouse, (or not to have one), a worldview, what personal philosophy and religion to embrace, (or to embrace none), how to relate to people, and more. We are bombarded with the need to make choices. How well we cope depends on how clearly we think.

Occasionally factors and events beyond our control significantly impact our lives. Things happen to us. But, to a much greater extent than we often admit, we mold our lives and control our future through the decisions we make. Other people make decisions that affect us, but we can always choose our response, and thus determine what happens next.

Although decision making is among the most frequent things we do and certainly among the **most important things we do**, we are not typically taught how to do it, nor do most of us consciously make an effort to learn to do it. We are presumably supposed to learn decision making by observation or through experience. Observing the results of others' decisions can be helpful, but observation, by itself, does not work well for learning to make decisions. And while experience, "the school of hard knocks", can provide useful lessons, as the sole method of learning it is very inefficient and often painful.

Important decisions, those that have significant ramifications for us and for others, warrant focused time and effort. Decision making is a critical life skill. Fortunately, it's a skill that can be learned and improved. We can learn to be better decision makers. Like learning to drive a car, it can be awkward at first, but we get more proficient with practice. To make better decisions, one has to *want* to learn and to grow in proficiency.

3

Not all decisions are of equal importance. Some influence our lives more than others. Decisions made today may impact our lives for years down the road. Choosing the wrong <u>vacation</u> may have minimal impact in the long run. Choosing the wrong <u>vocation</u> can make one's life miserable. Evaluating the importance of decisions is critical.

There are a few fundamental decisions that shape our lives. In this text, we will discuss seven:

- Who do I choose to be?
- How do I choose to see the world?
- How shall I live my life?
- What will I exclude from my life?
- How will I relate to other people?
- How will I contribute to humankind?
- What's it all about?

By design or default we all make these choices. There are no answers to these questions that are "right" for everyone, but there are principles and values that make some choices more effective than others.

Not all decisions are of a "yes or no", "black or white" type. Most important decisions involve shades of gray. Most must be made with less than all the information that could be relevant. Many must be made under time and/or other pressures. Some involve tradeoffs between conflicting objectives and rules. In spite of all these obstacles, learning to make the best choices possible, with the information and time available, is possible, and can be very rewarding.

Making wise decisions involves asking oneself a lot of fundamental questions, and honestly attempting to seek truthful and useful answers to those questions.

We can learn to make better decisions by: becoming more aware of their impact on our lives, taking responsibility for our decisions, consciously committing to improving them, developing a truthful and realistic understanding of the world within which we make decisions and employing an effective decision making <u>process</u>.

While the purpose of decision making is usually to produce positive results, outcomes are often uncertain. Even with the careful application of the best process, there is no guarantee that the results of a given decision will be positive. Good decisions can have negative consequences and poor decisions, by chance or luck, can be followed by great results. An evaluation of whether a decision was "good" or "bad" should relate, not just to the results, but to <u>how</u> the choice was made. Following an effective process will, in the long run, produce better results than knee jerk reactions and hap-hazard approaches.

Understand that no one makes <u>only</u> good decisions. Our objective should be, not to make "perfect" decisions every time, but to <u>make "better" decisions more often</u>, to increase the odds that the consequences will be positive. Following a systematic, logical process and consciously attempting to think rationally can help significantly.

An effective process + wisdom = better decisions. Better decisions = a better quality of life.

Important decisions can be tough and the consequences serious. Most of our more serious life problems are the result of poor decisions. Our prisons are full of people who made poor choices.

Many of our poor decisions are the result of not understanding *how* to make effective decisions. The quality of our decisions is determined not only by *what* we decide, but to a great extent by *how* we decide. The process is important. Using an effective process will not make tough decisions easy, but it will provide the assurance that we have given the issue our best effort and will increase the probability of a successful outcome.

Identify the key elements of the issue, gather relevant information, apply rigorous analysis and make the decision. The following is an outline of a systematic approach to improving decision making. Each of these elements will be described further in the remainder of the text.

1. FRAME THE ISSUE
2. IDENTIFY THE INFORMATION NEEDED TO MAKE A GOOD DECISION
3. IDENTIFY VIABLE OPTIONS/ALTERNATIVES
4. CONSIDER THE LIKELY CONSEQUENSES/RESULTS
5. CONSIDER THE IMPACT ON OTHERS
6. TEST THE ALTERNATIVES AGAINST YOUR VALUES
7. TEST THE ALTERNATIVES AGAINST YOUR GOALS AND OBJECTIVES
8. TUNE IN TO YOUR INTUITION
9. THINK IT THROUGH
10. MAKE A DECISION
11. IMPLEMENT IT
12. EVALUATE PAST DECISIONS

Should you consciously apply each of these steps to every decision you make? Of course not, life is too short. Part VII of the text outlines a variety of tools and procedures that have been found to be helpful for making effective decisions. Not all fit every decision or every decision maker. Certainly, one should not try to apply all of them to every decision. They are intended as aids, not rigid requirements.

The focus of this text is on improving the quality of critical, significant and important decisions. Through employing the process for those, you will come to naturally apply the principles and the mental discipline to your mundane, routine decisions and inevitably improve the quality of those as well.

The dominant excuse for not employing an effective process in decision making is the **"I don't have time"** rationalization. There is a lot of truth to the old adage that "you don't have time to do it right the first time, but you have (or will have to make) time to do it over again". The key is to match the time and effort you invest in the decision to the importance of the issue, and the potential impact of the consequences. Make the time to give important decisions the attention and effort they warrant.

Time can have a major impact on the quality of decisions. We rarely have all the time we would like for considering important decisions. Procrastination almost always has negative consequences. Putting off decisions until there is little time for analysis and thinking often leads to poor choices and may mean that the best alternatives are no longer available.

A Point to Ponder: Can you think of examples where failure to act has negative consequences?

While employing an effective process is very important, it is not the only determinant of the quality of decisions. **Of even greater importance is the wisdom we bring to the process.** Our knowledge, experience and mindsets have a significant impact on the effectiveness of our decisions In Parts II & III, we will discuss how the way we see the world, ourselves and our responsibilities affect our decisions. In Appendix Q of the text we will address: some important considerations of which we should be mindful, and some mental errors to avoid.

It's important to understand the interconnectivity of decisions. Decisions affect other decisions. The fundamental decisions we make about the really important elements of life: values, morals, goals and objectives, relationships, our worldviews, priorities and attitudes, all profoundly affect the other choices we make. Making effective decisions about these elements, lead to better choices in all aspects of our lives.

The focus of this text is to promote an understanding of how important decisions are to developing lives that are fulfilling and meaningful, and to present and encourage a comprehensive, and effective approach to decision making. Part IX attempts to pull it all together.

Guidelines about how to *live, love* and *learn* are offered throughout. This is not a book about does and don'ts. It is a book about THINKING. Inserts in the text, labeled "Points to Ponder, encourage the reader to think about some aspect of the topic being addressed.

We are the product of our decisions. Every important decision we make is an opportunity to impact the quality of our lives.

PART II

DEALING WITH LIFE SHAPING DECISIONS

The results of a few fundamental decisions go a long way toward shaping your life and your ability to live your time on earth with integrity, courage and meaning. Choosing to make these decisions consciously, and rationally thinking through the answers, significantly improves the probability that your life will be more meaningful, productive and satisfying, than if you simply react to what comes your way.

A. WHO DO YOU CHOOSE TO BE?

Who you want to be is largely your choice. We all have the opportunity and the responsibility to decide who we want to be. The decisions we make define who we are. When we know who we are and are comfortable with that understanding, we can live with purpose and meaning. Our "self" is unique and elastic. We have the ability to mold it to be what we consciously and sincerely want it to be, but we realize that potential only if we accept the responsibility and invest the effort to make it so.

I found the following on a plaque in a gift shop. I bought the plaque and mounted it along my "Ponder Path" in the woods behind our home, to remind me daily of what is important and that I am responsible for the meaning of my life:

LIVE THE LIFE YOU'VE
ALWAYS DREAMED OF.
BE FEARLESS IN THE FACE OF ADVERSITY.
RECOGNIZE THE BEAUTY
THAT SURROUNDS YOU.
NEVER STOP LEARNING.
REMEMBER WHERE YOU
CAME FROM, BUT DON'T
LOSE SIGHT OF WHERE
YOU ARE GOING.
USE YOUR IMAGINATION.
**THIS LIFE IS YOURS
TO CREATE.**

1. Select the Principles by Which You Will Live.

A life of meaning and satisfaction is based, not on material wealth, but on living a life aligned with the right principles. Principles are the value-based standards we use to decide how to act and react. Principles are matters of personal choice. Valid principles are not rules developed by a committee but are derived from the experiences of what has worked best for our species. They represent the time and experience tested collective wisdom of humankind. Examples of positive principles include: integrity, justice, compassion, accepting responsibility, generosity, self-control, meeting commitments, respect, love, and service.

2. Select Your Personal Values.

Core principles are based upon sound values. Making good decisions involves more than weighing facts and figures. The best decisions are not necessarily those which are the easiest, the most convenient, or the most personally beneficial. To make choices which are effective and with which we can live comfortably, our choices must be consistent with our core values. Values are those standards and qualities we deem to have inherent worth and which we consider deeply important. Decisions drive behavior. If our behavior is not consistent with our values, we will feel dissatisfied with the results, uncomfortable and out of sync with the world. When our actions are consistent with our values, we are much more likely to achieve positive outcomes and be more satisfied with our choices.

> "Carefully watch your thoughts, for they become your words. Manage and watch your words, for they become your actions. Consider and judge your actions, for they become your habits. Acknowledge and watch your habits, for they become your values. Understand and embrace your values, for they become your destiny."

> Mahatma Gandhi

Values are the foundation of character. Character determines self-respect and the respect with which we are regarded by others. Decisions about personal values are some of the most important decisions we ever make. They determine the kind of person we become. Once established, they should serve as guides for making other important decisions. Our values should provide an internal compass that guides the direction of our life journey. With every decision we make, we are writing the story of our lives. Strive to make yours a story of which you can be proud and which has meaning.

In thinking about the values that are important, we should consider the following questions:

- How do I define right and wrong?
- What do I consider to be my moral absolutes?
- How do I define ethics in dealing with people?
- What do I consider to be my basic personal responsibilities?

11

- What are the qualities I admire about people I respect?
- What makes me feel fulfilled and proud?
- What values were involved in decisions I regret?

The extent to which our lives have meaning is determined largely by our values. Our values define who we are and who we want to be. They often involve making choices about what is right and wrong and what is the responsible thing to do under the circumstances. To determine if a decision is "right", <u>we should test possible choices against our values</u>. To test a decision against our values, we must have previously considered and defined our ethical and moral standards and what core values are really important to us. That requires careful thought and is something that should be done with deliberation and great care, before we are faced with the pressure of making an important decision. By deciding <u>now</u> what is important, we will be better prepared to <u>align our actions with our values</u> in times of crisis or change.

Decisions about personal values are important. They deserve and require careful deliberation. To facilitate thinking about what values are important to you, consider completing the exercise in Appendix A.

This exercise takes time and careful consideration but is well worth the effort. Just conscientiously completing the exercise will improve the quality of your decisions, because it forces you to think about what is important to you.

Identifying, understanding and applying core values is an important part of an effective decision-making strategy. Becoming more aware of how critical values are in your life and applying them to the decisions you make will be useful for making choices that are effective, and about which you can feel confident.

"It is time to return to core values, time to get back to basics, to self-discipline and respect for the law, to consideration for others, to accepting responsibility for yourself and your family-and not shuffling it off on other people or the state."

John Major

Choose your core values, principles and ideals well. Express them through everything you do. The gift of free will is that we can choose our behaviors, we can choose to be evil or choose to be good. Figure out what is fundamental to who you want to be. Choose a course that results in peace of mind and self-respect. Do not compromise on the basics, but be very flexible about everything else.

"Values are principles and ideas that bring meaning to the seemingly mundane experience of life. A meaningful life that ultimately brings happiness and pride requires you to respond to temptation, as well as challenges, with honor, dignity and courage"

Laura Schlessinger

3. Develop Your Character

Character development, the transition from a preoccupation with self, to consciousness of and caring for others, is an important element of personal growth. Our characters define who we are as persons. Character determines how we respond to the events and circumstances in our lives. How we respond determines the results of those encounters.

"What lies behind us and what lies before us are small matters compared to what lies within us."

Oliver Wendell Holmes

One's worth as an individual is determined by character, not by titles, educational degrees, possessions or wealth. Character is influenced by genes, experiences, examples and education, but is largely determined by judgement, discretion and personal choices. Character is malleable, we get to choose which traits we want to develop and emphasize. Our "self" is elastic. We can mold it if we so choose. A person of "strong" character is one who is moral and ethical, does what is right in spite of personal gain or hardship, cares about people and can be trusted.

Character defines who we are. In the final analysis, what we are determines the worth, the effectiveness, of our lives and communicates what we value much more eloquently than anything we say. Our character is defined by the principles by which we conduct our lives. Many generations of multiple cultures have demonstrated that there are basic **principles** for effective living, and that people can be truly successful and happy only if they learn to integrate those principles into their basic characters. The shaping of character is based upon the fundamental idea that there are certain principles that govern human decency and effectiveness, natural laws in the human dimension that are just as real as natural laws in the physical dimension, (such as the law of gravity).

These principles and values are the foundation on which we should each erect the structure of our characters:

a. **Morality & Ethics** - Not all decisions involve moral choices. Choosing the restaurant at which to have lunch is morally neutral. Others, such as decisions about whether to lie, cheat or steal, can have profound consequences. Those that force us to consider what is "right and wrong" can be challenging. There is more to determining if a decision is the "right" one, than deciding that it solves the problem, resolves the issue or maximizes personal benefit. To be "right", a decision must not only meet our objectives, but also be moral and ethical.

> "So, I think ethics is a broader thing that's less focused on prohibitions and is more about looking at principles, questions and ideas about how to live your life".

> Peter Singer

Morality is about how we treat people. Right decisions are those that resolve our issues, while demonstrating respect for peoples' rights and concern for peoples' needs. "Right" decisions treat people fairly and with decency.

b. **Honesty/Integrity** - connotes not cheating, lying or stealing. Honesty is the foundation for trust, which is essential to cooperation and interpersonal relationships.

> "Integrity is congruence between what you know, what you profess, and what you do."

> Nathaniel Branden

> "I hope I shall possess firmness and virtue enough to maintain what I consider the most enviable of all titles, the character of an honest man."

> George Washington

Coach John Wooden relates that he received what proved to be valuable wisdom from his father's "two sets of threes":

> Never lie.
> Never cheat.
> Never steal.

15

Don't whine.
Don't complain.
Don't make excuses.

c. **True/Truth** – We typically think of true as the opposite of false and truth as the opposite of a lie. While these understandings are accurate, they are not complete. The concepts are multi-dimensional. Certainly, we should speak only the truth. What we say reflects who we are. Lying is destructive to relationships. Statements, contentions, facts cannot be both true and false, as those of us who have taken true/false quizzes in school can attest. But there's more to the concepts:

- True can mean straight, or perfectly square, as in a carpenter constructing a door frame so that the door will open and close properly. A carpenter may use a "plumb bob" or a "square" to determine what is "true'. It is unfortunate that we don't have such a tool for telling us if what we hear and read is "true"
- True can mean "real", as in; he is a "true" friend.
- True can mean "exemplary", as in: he is a "true" gentleman.
- True can mean "demonstrable", as in: ice melts at temperatures above 32 degrees F.
- True can mean "actual" as opposed to imaginary, as in; "true story" publications.
- True can mean "valuable", meaningful" or "useful" when referring to the message in a story that is not necessarily factual.

Black Elk, a famous and oft quoted Sioux Medicine Man, when commenting upon one of the myths of his people, stated:

> "…this they tell, and whether it happened or not, I do not know, but if you think about it, you will see that it

16

is true."

All of these dimensions of truth have relevance to how we live our lives. Living truthfully means not telling lies, but much more. It means being true to who we want to be and what we want to do. We should be true, real, to others, and more importantly, true to ourselves, true to our values and to what we "know" is right.

> "I prefer to be true to myself, even at the hazard
> of incurring the ridicule of others, rather than be
> false, and to incur my own abhorrence."

> William Douglass

What is true for us may change. The world changes. We change. What was true for us at age ten is not the same as what is true for us at age 80. That is not a bad thing. It is inevitable. We've had more experiences, learned more. Our circumstances have changed.

Seek the truth. Think it through.

d. **Respect for Human Dignity** - the concept that all persons have intrinsic worth and certain "unalienable rights", which we must honor if we expect to enjoy those same rights.

e. **Compassion** - People matter. We should be ever aware of the impact of our actions, words and decisions on others. Almost all our decisions affect other people. We should treat people with dignity and respect. Things are to be used, people are to be loved. Loving things and using people inevitably lead to poor consequences. We should understand that part of our reason for being is to help lighten the burdens of others.

f. **Kindness** – The attribute of kindness encompasses being attentive, considerate, generous, empathetic and friendly. It involves listening to and helping others. It means celebrating the successes of others and sharing their woes. It is an interpersonal skill that engenders trust and strengthens relationships. It means showing others in a multitude of little ways that you care.

> "Constant kindness can accomplish much. As the sun makes ice to melt, kindness causes misunderstanding, mistrust and hostility to evaporate."

> Albert Schweitzer

g. **Accept Responsibility** - We are each responsible for who we are, what we do, what we say, how we treat people and how we live our lives. We are responsible for the consequences of our decisions. Accept personal responsibility.

> "People are always blaming their circumstances for what they are. I don't believe in circumstances. The people who get on in this world are the people who get up and look for the circumstances they want, and if they can't find them, make them."

> George Bernard Shaw

In his book, *TAKING RESPONSIBILITY*, Nathaniel Branden, a PhD Psychologist, suggests that we start each day with two questions: "What's good in my life? and What needs to be done? The first question keeps us focused on the positives, The second reminds us that our life and well-being are our own responsibility and keeps us proactive."

h. **Conscientiousness** - Studies have shown that one trait shared by those of high achievement and happiness is conscientiousness.

"Conscientiousness is emerging as one of the primary determinants of successful functioning across the lifespan."

Paul Tough

Literally, being conscientious means following one's conscience, doing what is right. Developing a sound value system and living those values is important.

Conscientiousness also means more. Being conscientious means being dependable, doing what you say you will do and being there for others, demonstrating that others can count on you. Being conscientious means being aware of, and responsive to, the needs of others.

"Good luck is the willing handmaiden of an upright character and the   conscientious observance of duty".

Russell Lowell

Being conscientious also means caring about the quality of what one does. We do not have to be perfect or do things perfectly, but setting high standards and striving to meet them leads to greater satisfaction and achievement and earns the respect of others.

Be conscientious. It will help you fulfill your responsibilities to others and enhance how you feel about yourself and what you do.

"Being conscientious is like brushing your teeth. It prevents problems."

Brent Roberts

i. **Self-Control** - Impulsive, irrational behaviors can result in poor decisions that: are harmful to personal health and well-being, can impair personal effectiveness and can damage relationships.

> "Self-control is the chief element in self-respect, and self-respect is the chief element in courage."

> Thucydides

j. **Fairness/Justice** - Fairness is the principle upon which our whole system of justice is based and the foundation for our understanding of what is "right". Justice is the principle upon which right relationships are built. Treat others fairly and have the courage to oppose injustice. Injustice often prevails, not because everyone approves, but because few have the courage to openly disapprove.

k. **Quality/Excellence** - Whatever we do, we should do it well. Perfection is not possible but striving for perfection makes a difference.

l. **Do No Harm** – The most basic principle of all is that of not harming others. It includes not attempting to control or manipulate others, not trying to manage their affairs.

m. **Meet Commitments** – Demonstrating that we always do what we say we will do earns us the trust and respect of others and a clear conscience. Failing to meet commitments betrays others and ourselves.

> "Resolve to perform what you ought; perform without fail what you resolve."

> Benjamin Franklin

n. **Demonstrate Courage** - Courage is not the absence of fear. Demonstrating courage means doing what is right regardless of criticism, personal hardship, or popular opinion. Demonstrating courage includes confronting and attempting to correct injustice and unfairness.

20

"Keep strong, if possible. In any case, keep cool. Have unlimited patience. Never corner an opponent, and always assist him to save face. Put yourself in his shoes – so as to see things through his eyes. Avoid self-righteousness like the devil – nothing is so self-blinding.

B. H. Liddell Hart

Being a person of strong character means knowing what to do, being willing to do it and actually doing it. It means having the integrity to refuse to do what is wrong and having the courage to do what is right.

These principles are guidelines for human conduct that have been proven to have enduring, intrinsic value. Integrating them into our characters will make our lives richer, more effective and more satisfying. We should practice them, make them habits, and pass them on. Of all the variables that determine how we live our lives, character matters most. Character is the bedrock that enables us to deal effectively with the circumstances and challenges of life. Mold it well and it will serve you well.

4. Know Yourself

The ways of thinking about decision making outlined herein encourage you to consider who you are and who you want to be, to ponder your values and your priorities, to determine what gives your life meaning and what gives you particular satisfaction. If you have pet peeves, if you tend to have particular fears, acknowledge them and reflect on how they might be affecting your choices. All these factors are elements of self-knowledge which impact decision making.

"It takes courage to grow up and become who you really are."

E.E. Cummings

The more clearly we understand our strengths and weaknesses, our values and what we want from life, the more effective our choices will be. Know what you want and don't want. When gathering information for making decisions, don't overlook relevant information about the decision maker (you). Get to know yourself. If you are dissatisfied with what you find, think about the qualities you admire in people you respect most, (living or dead). Reflect on those qualities and emulate them.

"I found power in accepting the truth of who I am. It may not be a truth that others can accept, but I cannot live any other way. How would it be to live a lie every minute of your life?"

Alison Goodman

The essence of rationality is respect for the facts of reality. The fact is you have needs, motives, emotions, beliefs, mental states, goals, ambitions, and feelings. To function effectively, you need to be conscious of both external and internal realities. Make self-awareness a conscious element of your decision-making process.

Consider the standards by which you measure the effectiveness of your decisions. Make sure they are realistic and relevant. Self-knowledge can help you achieve your goals. Make sure those goals are worthy, are yours, not someone else's, and not what you think society wants you to be.

We all have fears. Fear is not all bad. Some fears help keep us alive. Fears that facilitate self-preservation are functional. Fears of the unknown are often irrational and crippling. Seeking positive, but unfamiliar, new relationship and

22

experiences can help us grow and learn. Fears rooted in selfishness distort reality. Fears driven by motives of greed, control and insecurity are dysfunctional. They impede effective decision making. Identify and categorize your fears and examine them for validity.

> "Courage is resistance to fear, mastery of fear - not absence of fear."

> Mark Twain

Making the right decision sometimes takes courage. We develop courage by facing our fears, examining their causes and rationality, and doing what is right in spite of them.

Acquiring the skill to choose our attitudes, to choose our thoughts and to choose what actions we take may be the most critical skills we can develop. Self–knowledge is fundamental to developing those skills. Know thyself.

> "I learned that courage was not the absence of fear, but the triumph over it. The brave man is not he who does not feel afraid, but he who conquers that fear."

> Nelson Mandela

To help you with the process of understanding yourself, complete the worksheet in Appendix B. A second copy of the worksheet is included as Appendix C. Fill it out a year from now and compare it to the one you complete now, to see if there have been any changes to your self-perception.

5. Recognize Your Self Worth

How we see ourselves matters. Our perceptions of self can severely limit who we are and who we can become, or can unchain and inspire us to be what we decide to be.

We must be very careful of "labels" we assign to ourselves or that are affixed to us by others. If we see ourselves as "poor at math", we will not do well in math. If we see ourselves as "dishonest", we are likely to steal. If we see ourselves as "disabled", we will act out our perception of what disabled means. If we see ourselves as "a victim of a broken home", we will act like a victim. If we believe labels assigned by others: lazy, dumb, clumsy, we are likely to act as labeled.

If we see ourselves as capable, caring and worthy, we are much more likely to achieve. We can choose not to be prisoners of our history, our environment or the perceptions of others.

We inevitably judge ourselves. I have no idea who you will be, but of one thing I am certain, you will not be perfect. You will make mistakes. You will make poor decisions. Everyone does. Don't beat yourself up for your imperfections. Examine and learn from your mistakes, so you don't repeat them and so you develop insights that will help you make better decisions in the future.

B. HOW SHOULD YOU RELATE TO OTHER PEOPLE?

1. Recognize That We are All Related

In thinking about relationships, it is important to understand and appreciate that we are all related. There is an increasing, but by no means universal, awareness that we are, at a very basic level, all connected and interdependent. This understanding has significant implications.

One of the more unique aspects of traditional Native American culture is the depth of understanding and appreciation of the interconnectedness and interdependence of all people and all things. This concept was often expressed with the phrase: "we are all related". In the Lakota and Dakota cultures, prayers were often concluded with the phrase "for all my relations", the

24

meaning of which included: family, tribe, all the nations of two leggeds in the world, the four leggeds, the winged creatures and all the earth's living things.

Native Americans were not the first to understand this truth. In the 6th century BCE, the Buddha said:

> "The practice of making others happy is based upon the clear understanding of life, which is Oneness. In deep gratitude, let us realize this Oneness of all life, the heart of which is compassion."

In the first century CE, a Stoic philosopher wrote:

> "All that you behold, that which comprises both god and man, is one – we are the parts of one great body."
>
> Seneca

This concept that everything within the universe is living and related has moral implications. It means that we each have a responsibility to care for all living things, for maintaining balance and harmony in the world, and demonstrating respect for all things that live. Because we are all related, we should strive to live in harmony with all people and all living things.

> "You cannot get through a single day without having an impact on the world around you. What you do makes a difference, and you have to decide what kind of difference you want to make."
>
> Jane Goodall

In the book *GROUNDED*, published in 2015, Diana Butler Bass uses these words to explain the 'Big Bang' theory of creation:

> "The big bang's simplest insight, and the one with the most profound implications for understanding God and

contemporary spirituality, is straightforward: everything that exists was created at the same time; thus, all things are connected by virtue of being made of the same matter. This dust (matter) has, throughout time, formed and reformed into gases, worlds and living beings......According to this scientific theory, everything is connected with everything else. Quite literally, Human Beings, (and everything else) are made of stardust."

In her book *THE SACRED DEPTHS OF NATURE,* Ursula Goodenough, one of America's premier biologists, states the following:

"So, all the creatures on the planet today share a huge number of genetic ideas. Most of my genes are like most gorilla genes, but they're also like many of the genes in a mushroom. I have more genes than a mushroom, to be sure, and some critical genes are certainly different, but the important piece to take in here is our deep interrelatedness, our deep genetic homology, with the rest of the living world."

Goodenough p 72.

Scientists are not the only group of moderns who have embraced this concept of interrelatedness. In a book titled *PROCESS THEOLOGY,* Bruce G. Epperly lists the following among what he labels as the "Essential Concepts of Process Theology":

- *"All living things exist in relationship with one another.* We live in an interdependent universe in which each moment of experience arises from its environment, whose influence provides both limits and possibilities."
- *"Experience is universal, though variable, and extends beyond humankind.* While creatures differ in

complexity and impact on the world, every creature has some minimal level of responsiveness to its environment."

- *"The universality of experience leads to the recognition that every creature is inherently valuable and deserves moral consideration.*
- *Process Theology values all creation, even apart from its impact on human life… flora and fauna are valuable not just because we appreciate their beauty but because they experience some level of joy and sorrow. They matter to God and, accordingly, should enter into our own moral calculations."*

In his book; *A SEEKER'S THEOLOGY,* John Macort, a retired Episcopal Priest who taught in Catholic schools and later became a practicing Quaker, wrote:

"We are all related as we share that divine Existence with God. We are all united as One.

In his book, *ETERNAL LIFE: A NEW VISION,* John Shelby Spong wrote:

"In fact, we now know that all matter within our universe, from the farthest star to the content of your body and mine is interconnected. Such a sense of interdependency has, before our time, never even been imagined. Human life is kin not just to the great apes but to the cabbages and indeed even to the plankton in the sea… That insight leads to the conclusion that while separation may have been our perception, it is not the law of the universe. A deep interrelated unity is."

Despite their differences in perspective, scientists and theologians are reaching the same conclusions as did the Indigenous People of this continent - every living thing is interconnected and interdependent - We Are All Related.

Our world would be an immeasurably better place, a place of balance, harmony and peace, if we could learn to treat all humans as brothers and sisters and all living things as sacred, and thus worthy of respect.

2. Be Inclusive vs Exclusive

Some of our most important decisions involve how we view and relate to other people. One of the greatest sources of strife, conflict, suffering and inhumanity in the world, today and historically, is humankind's attitude toward, and reaction to, differences in: race, religion and culture. Unconscionable atrocities have been committed against fellow humans because they looked, thought, believed and/or prayed differently than the perpetrators. These atrocities were the result of personal and collective decisions.

> "I happen to think that the singular evil of our time is prejudice. It is from this evil that all other evils grow and multiply."
>
> Rod Sterling

The all-too-common reactions to personal differences are: fear, mistrust and misunderstanding. What we desperately need is an awareness of, an appreciation of, and a commitment to, genuine, inclusive community, with the term community encompassing family, neighborhood, country, and world. We are all in this together, whether we realize it or not. No matter how much we value our independence, we are mutually dependent.

> "You're not under attack when others gain rights and privileges you've always had."
>
> DaShanne Stokes

"The way to be successful is to find a way to be inclusive of everybody.

It's the difference between an attitude that looks at diversity and assumes you can be successful despite it, versus an attitude that looks at diversity and assumes you can be successful as a result of it."

"Magic" Johnson

Tolerance or Acceptance - Intolerance is despicable, but tolerance is insufficient. We need to do more than tolerate those unlike us. The difference between tolerance and acceptance is huge. "I tolerate" means I consider myself superior to, but I will allow the existence of, others as long as they do not impinge on my own life and way of doing things, or encroach on my value systems. To simply tolerate means to barely notice that others who are different exist and to have as little as possible to do with them.

"The world is getting too small for both an Us and a Them. Us and Them have become codependent, intertwined, fixed to one another. We have no separate fates, but are bound together in one. And our fear of one another is the only thing capable of our undoing."

Sam Killermann

To accept others is to place ourselves on the same level, so as to know the other, to allow the other the same rights that we expect, and to attempt to understand each other, despite any differences. It means respecting another's right to be different and to attempt to learn by really listening to the perspectives of others.

A Point to Ponder: Have you personally witnessed examples of prejudice and discrimination? How did it make you feel?

When we speak of inclusiveness, we are not talking about uniformity, but about a mindset that values and celebrates differences. Humans desperately need community. A group based on exclusivity is not a community, but a clique. Real communities are inclusive.

> "Inclusion works to the advantage of everyone. We all have things to learn and we all have something to teach."
>
> Helen Henderson

"Love your neighbor as yourself" is a quotation usually associated with Christianity, but the closely related "do unto others as you would have them do unto you" is a basic value common to many cultures. Living these values is a personal responsibility and should be incorporated into all personal and group relationships.

I noticed the following on a poster in a church window. I thought it so relevant that I parked the car and went back and copied it down:

LOVE YOUR NEIGHBOR WHO DOESN'T
LOOK LIKE YOU
THINK LIKE YOU
LOVE LIKE YOU
SPEAK LIKE YOU
PRAY LIKE YOU
VOTE LIKE YOU
LOVE YOUR NEIGHBOR,
NO EXCEPTIONS

Values and principles are learned, primarily from family and friends. Children are not born with exclusivity, intolerance and bigotry built in. They have to be taught. In the early 1950's, Rogers and Hammerstein expressed this truth through the words of a song in the score of the musical *SOUTH PACIFIC*:

> "they have to be taught before it's too late
> before they are six or seven or eight
> to hate all the people their relatives hate.
> They have to be carefully taught."

We must carefully teach young people inclusiveness, acceptance and respect for human dignity. As with most values, we most effectively teach these by example.

Being an inclusive person means:

- Communicating honestly with each other
- Respecting and celebrating human differences
- Transcending differences rather than attempting to obliterate them
- Genuinely demonstrating an interest in the values, beliefs and worldviews of others
- Showing empathy – the willingness to share the burdens of others.
- Building relationships that go deeper than superficial niceties
- Committing to: understand each other, rejoice together, mourn together and find delight in each other.

A Point to Ponder: Seek out and learn from those who are "different". Make a personal decision to embrace inclusiveness. List in Appendix D, some of the things you can personally do to promote inclusiveness.

"We need to give each other space so that we may both give and receive such beautiful things as ideas, openness, dignity, joy, healing, and inclusion."

Max de Pree

3. Develop Meaningful Relationships and Friendships.

Relationships Matter! They enrich our lives. How then should we treat them?

a. **Cherish Family** – Relationships with family members can at times be challenging. But ties to family are extremely important. It is typically from family that we initially learn values and develop a worldview. We should: value family, make family a priority, always be there for family, provide support when needed, be loyal to family, enjoy family, create and nurture family traditions and strengthen and nurture family relationships. Keep in mind that family members are human and not infallible. They make mistakes. When yours make mistakes, forgive them, but don't copy them.

> "What do most people say on their deathbeds? They don't say 'I wish I had made more money'. What they say is: 'I wish I had spent more time with my family'".

> David Rubenstein

One of the things I respect most about my Amish friends is their commitment to family. They don't send kids to orphanages or their old folks to nursing homes, to be cared for by strangers. They take care of their young and their old. Family is important. Family assumes responsibility for family.

32

"The only things that are really permanent are love, family and friendship. At the end of the day, that's what it really boils down to. The rest is just stuff."

Jared Kushner

b. Friendship - Friendship is a very special kind of relationship. Being a friend means giving of oneself. We all need friends. A friend is someone who can sense what a friend needs and is ever willing to help meet that need. Making friends and keeping friends is not always easy. You have to want to be a friend and work at it. The way to <u>have</u> the kinds of friends you want and need; is to <u>be</u> the kind of friend you want to have.

- Be a good listener and don't try to dominate conversations. People often need to "unload", to air their concerns and problems. Having someone they can trust to share their burdens is a real asset.
- Never attempt to persuade a friend to do something that is inconsistent with her/his values or ethics.
- Take the initiative. Demonstrate that you wish to be friendly. People often confuse reticence with arrogance.
- Demonstrate real interest in the friend's life and what interests him/her.
- Be slow to judge. Be willing to get to know a person's true character.
- Be willing to forgive small mistakes. Don't expect friends to be perfect, but set limits. Don't criticize. Criticism destroys relationships.
- Be loyal to friends. Don't criticize them behind their backs or break confidences.
- Act like you want your friends to act.

- Keep promises.
- Perform small acts of kindness.
- When you make a mistake, say "I'm sorry".
- Encourage friends to be their best and support their positive efforts.

When choosing friends, (recognize that it is your choice), apply the above as criteria. While true friends are important, don't make friends the center of your life. Friends are human and imperfect. Don't let them control who you are. Choose friends based on character, not wealth, social status or popularity. The test of true friends is whether or not you are a better person when you are with them. Choose well.

There are certain principles that have proven effective for making relationships work:

1) **Earn Trust** - Trust is the foundation of all effective relationships. In THE SPEED OF TRUST, Stephen M. R. Covey wrote:

> "There is one thing that is common to every individual, relationship, team, family, organization, nation, economy, and civilization throughout the world - one thing which, if removed, will destroy the most powerful government: the most successful business, the most thriving economy, the most influential leadership, the greatest friendship, the strongest character, the deepest love. On the other hand, if developed and leveraged, that one thing has the potential to create unparalleled success and prosperity in every dimension of life. Yet, it is the least understood, most neglected, and most underestimated possibility of our time. That one thing is trust."

Trust is built on integrity and competence. Trust must be earned. We earn trust by meeting commitments, by telling the truth, and doing what we say we are going to do. Being trustworthy means that those with whom we interact are confident of our motives, our ethics, our reliability and our abilities.

Trust is crucial. EARN IT!

2) **Be Real** – To develop meaningful relationships requires that we be real, that we drop   pretenses and reveal our true feelings and our true selves. Being authentic means admitting that you are a work in progress and are not perfect. It means being genuinely empathetic.

A key lesson in life is to understand our real selves, to be real in our relationships and to see the authenticity in others.

3) **Demonstrate Respect** - Effective people have well established standards and expectations for personal relationships. Principles for relationships are based upon assumptions of mutual respect. Some of the principles considered necessary for achieving harmonious relationships are as follow:

- Always tell the truth. Lying destroys relationships
- Listen carefully.
- Never interrupt when another is talking.
- Seek to understand. Visualize yourself in the other person's "shoes".
- Be honest.
- Keep commitments.
- Accept responsibility for your words and actions.

4) **Think Win/Win** - Many significant decisions involve
   interactions with others. Stephen Covey contends that
   to make these decisions effective, they should be
   constructed as "Win/Win".

> "Win/Win is a frame of mind and heart that
> constantly seeks mutual benefit in human
> interactions. Win/Win means that agreements or
> solutions are mutually beneficial, mutually
> satisfying. With Win/Win solutions, all parties
> feel good about the decision and feel committed
> to the action plan."

Covey continues:

> "Win/Win is based on the paradigm that there is
> plenty for everybody, that one person's success
> is not achieved at the expense or exclusion of
> the success of others. Win/Win is a belief in the
> Third Alternative. It's not your way or my way;
> it's a better way, a higher way."

Not all relationships are amicable. Most of us hold on to old
grudges and nurse real and imagined wounds that refuse to
heal. There are some persons that we find offensive. We need
to pay attention to those relationships as well as those with
friends. When Lincoln's advisors protested that he was
supposed to destroy his enemies, rather than befriend them, he
replied, "Am I not destroying my enemies when I make friends
of them?"

Each of us is the common denominator in all of our
relationships. The attitude that we bring to the relationship
determines the quality thereof. Every relationship, no matter
how brief, is potentially important because it may alter
someone's life.

A Point to Ponder: Friends have influence with friends. Be sure the influence you wield is positive. There are some things you should not say to or do to friends. List some of them in Appendix E.

When you have a true friend, let the friend know how important that friendship is to you.

PART III.

CHOOSING HOW TO VIEW THE WORLD.

Our perceptions of how the world functions and what is important, particularly our perceptions about people, affect the decisions we make and our satisfaction with life. The more accurate one's worldview, the closer it aligns with reality, the better one's decisions will be and the more stable one's life will be. There are many facets to a personal worldview. The concept includes one's knowledge, philosophy, attitudes, principles, values, emotions, morality, ethics, biases and more. It includes one's perspective about what really matters, the purpose and meaning of life, assumptions about how the world really works, about how we interpret experiences and our responsibilities to others.

The following are observations about some of the more important elements of a worldview, elements that should be given serious thought, because they can have a huge impact on choices, life outcomes and one's satisfaction with life.

A. HUMAN NATURE and HUMAN RIGHTS

Philosophers have for centuries, with no consensus, debated the issue of whether humankind is basically good and altruistic or basically selfish and evil. We will not attempt to resolve that debate, but focus on what assumptions lead to the most effective decisions. Someone who views people as basically "good" and of inherent worth will make different decisions than one who views people as inherently "evil" and out to take advantage of me. I personally prefer the conclusions of Mencius, a Chinese philosopher of the Confucian school, who contended that humans have four basic tendencies:

1. A sense of compassion that develops into benevolence.

2. A sense of shame and distain that develops into righteousness.
3. A sense of respect and courtesy that develops into propriety.
4. A sense of right and wrong that develops into wisdom.

> "Therefore, humans have the capacity to be good, even though they are not all good."

I like the idea that we have the capacity to be good, but have to choose to exercise that capacity. For decision making, I suggest that it is appropriate to recognize that all others have that capacity, and until experience indicates otherwise, assume that they have chosen to exercise it.

We should also recognize that all humans have the right to "life, liberty and the pursuit of happiness" and the right to be treated with dignity and respect.

B. POSITIVE or NEGATIVE

Seeing a glass as half full instead of half empty is more than a platitude. It indicates how we see the world, and how we see the world affects the way we live your lives.

> *"If you concentrate on finding whatever is good in every situation, you will discover that your life will suddenly be filled with gratitude, a feeling that nurtures the soul."*

> Rabbi Harold Kushner

"Positive Thinking" has gotten a lot of ink since Norman Vincent Peale published his book, *The Power of Positive Thinking,* in 1952. The concept is dismissed by some as unrealistically "looking at the world through rose colored glasses" and ignoring the negative aspects of life. That is unfortunate because it really means dealing with life's challenges with a positive attitude. It means trying to see the good in other people, considering yourself and your capabilities as worthy and attempting to make the best of bad situations.

Studies have shown that those with positive attitudes toward life are typically healthier and happier than those with negative attitudes. These are real benefits, and recent research indicates that there are also positive implications for decision making.

Psychological research at the University of North Carolina demonstrated that experiencing positive thoughts and emotions enabled participants to visualize and articulate more possibilities and alternatives than did those with negative thoughts and emotions. This has implications for the process of searching for alternatives and options when making decisions. The same research also indicates that a positive attitude helps one build skill sets (like decision making and problem solving skills), that have long range benefits.

A Point to Ponder: Have you ever witnessed someone incurring negative consequences because of a negative attitude?

A positive mindset makes you feel better and helps you make better choices. Think Positively!

C. SCARCITY or ABUNDANCE

The concepts of Scarcity and Abundance Mindsets were, if not coined, at least widely publicized by Stephen Covey in his best-selling book THE 7 HABITS OF HIGHLY EFFECTIVE PEOPLE. Covey wrote:

> "Most people are deeply scripted in what I call the Scarcity Mentality. They see life as having only so much, as though there was only one pie out there, and if

40

someone else were to get a big piece of the pie, it would mean less for everybody else. The Scarcity Mentality is a zero-sum paradigm of life."

Those with a Scarcity Mindset are convinced that there is simply not enough to go around. Their perception is that if they are to get "more", they have to take it away from someone else. If someone else gets "more", that means there is "less" for them. The scarcity mindset focuses on the short term and ignores the long term. It fosters selfishness and competitiveness rather than collaboration. It creates feelings of jealousy and sadness at another's success or gain.

About the Abundance Mindset, Covey wrote:

> "The Abundance Mindset, on the other hand, flows from a deep inner sense of personal worth and security. It is the paradigm that there is plenty out there and enough to spare for everybody. It results in the sharing of prestige, of recognition, of profits, of decision making. It opens possibilities, options, alternatives and creativity."

Peter Diamandis and Steven Kotler in their book, appropriately titled ABUNDANCE, convincingly contend that the Scarcity Mentality is not only fallacious, but effectively stifles creativity, as well as solutions to significant world problems. It is a self-fulfilling mindset. The beliefs that: the hole is too deep to climb out of, the problems are too big to solve, the trends are worsening instead of improving, cause many to give up hope, and thus these beliefs get in the way of finding effective solutions. They foster an attitude of "why should I care, the world is going to hell anyway".

The authors point out that because we are hard wired to be alert to, and respond instinctively to, threats (a condition necessary for the survival of our ancestors) and because we are constantly bombarded with "bad news" (bad news sells papers and airtime), we have a negative cognitive bias – the tendency to give more weight to negative information and experiences than positive ones. "The inability of people to see the positive trends through the sea of bad news – that may be the biggest stumbling block on the road toward abundance."

Diamandis and Kotler argue that the world's major problems are solvable. What it takes is a different way of framing the issues and visualizing solutions.

There is plenty of "good" for everyone. Resolve to be a part of the solution, not a part of the problem. Think WIN/WIN! Think ABUNDANCE!

D. WHO is in CONTROL?

You can choose to view yourself as a helpless <u>victim</u> of circumstances and the whims of others, or as <u>master</u> of your fate. There is a lot of truth to the old adage that "If it is to be, it is up to me". Lots of research indicates that those who take personal responsibility for their lives are more successful and happier than those who attribute their life consequences to external forces.

The findings of noted clinical psychologist Julian Rotter indicate that where one perceives oneself on a continuum of internal, verses external, control significantly influences the decisions one makes, and thus one's personal attainment, success, and happiness. Those operating on the <u>internal control</u> end of the spectrum experience the most positive results. He found that people with a more internal sense of control:

- Are more likely to engage in activities that improve their circumstances.
- Work harder to develop knowledge, skills and abilities.

42

- Are more inquisitive and analytical in evaluating outcomes.
- Are more focused on achievement.
- Tend to work harder and persevere longer
- Learn more from their experiences, which they then apply to future situations.

This does not mean that you can have total control. Things will happen to you over which you have no control, but you always have control of how you chose to respond to those factors. Whenever tempted to think that some person or something is "ruining your life", look in the mirror. It is almost always you doing the ruining. Playing the "victim" is a disastrous way to go through life.

Recognize that you always have a choice and that choosing not to choose is a choice in itself. Developing your decision making and problem-solving skills enhances your control. Don't let circumstances and other people control your life.

E. CHANGE

Change is not a four-letter word! Embrace, don't attempt to avoid, change; provided the change is positive. Some contend that resistance to change is human nature. That is a cop-out. Change almost always involves effort. Some fear that change will mean loss of control. Fear and reluctance to make the effort are what generate resistance to change. To accomplish worthwhile results, you have to invest personal effort, overcome your own fears and help others do the same.

Everything in life changes. Everything! Change is another word for evolution. *How* we evolve is our choice. *That* we evolve is not. Life is a process of continuous change. The world is constantly changing. If we don't change, we lose touch with reality. Learning changes (expands, alters) our minds. Change is how we grow. The sum total of human knowledge is doubling roughly every ten years. If we don't learn to adapt to changes, we become obsolete.

> "Progress is impossible without change and those who cannot change their minds, cannot change anything."

Bernard Shaw

F. FAIRNESS & JUSTICE

Don't expect the world and life to be fair and just. They are not. But you can be and should be, thus making the world and life a little fairer and more just.

Fairness and justice embrace the concepts of doing what is "right", what is consistent with accepted standards of conduct, what is impartial and non-discriminatory.

These terms also have subtle, and not so subtle, nuances and interpretations that can at times conflict, and cause conflicts. "Fair" to some means equal, as in everyone should be treated equally. To others it may mean that everyone should get what they deserve, as in rewards should be related to effort. Those who produce/contribute more should get more. Those who are lazy and shiftless should get less. Still another perspective is that fairness means fulfilling one's responsibilities to those in society with the greatest needs. That those who have more have an obligation to give more to those who have less. How to do the fair and just thing is not always crystal clear. We must try anyway. Think about it.

Don't expect life to be fair or that justice will always prevail. The history of this country and the world is replete with injustice, especially for those who are "different". Some contend that the fact that 30% of Americans are people of color, yet 60% of the population of the nation's prisons are people of color, is an indication that the justice "system" is biased.

The Euro-American justice system is based upon principles of punishment and retribution. The underlying logic is that, because the offender has caused a victim to suffer, the offender should be made to suffer. It is an adversarial system designed to satisfy the victim's and society's desire for revenge.

Some Eastern cultures and the Indigenous People of this continent had/have a different approach for dealing with justice. The focus is upon the restoration of balance and harmony between the offended and the offender, and the offender and the community. The emphasis is on mending. The objective is to make amends and restore relationships.

In personal relationships, seeking balance and harmony and practicing the golden rule are more effective than seeking revenge or "getting even".

It is in no way "fair" that some are born with physical limitations/defects, that some contract debilitating diseases and others stay healthy, that some of us are obese and waste food, while thousands of children die every day from starvation and malnutrition.

Bad things do happen to good people. The fact is: life is not fair, is not just, that our systems of justice are imperfect. In spite of all that, we should personally strive to be fair and just and to do everything we can to promote fairness and justice.

G. WORK

How we view work has a lot to do with our comfort level with life. If we view work as punishment, drudgery, a necessary evil, the price we have to pay to make a living, chances are we will: not do it very well, will derive little satisfaction from it

45

and will find our lives full of stress. If we don't do it very well, it is not likely to impress those to whom we are responsible. That will inevitably lead to more stress.

"Work done for a reward is much lower than work done in the Yoga of wisdom. Set thy heart upon the work, but never on its reward. Work not for the reward; but never cease to do thy work."

The Bhagavad Gita

If we view work as a challenge, an opportunity to learn, grow, and demonstrate our abilities to do "good" work, it can be a source of pride, self-esteem and satisfaction. No matter the level of responsibility, even if it is sweeping streets, doing well what we do is important; emotionally, psychologically and monetarily.

A positive perspective about work increases effectiveness, peace of mind and satisfaction.

PART IV.

CHOOSING HOW TO LIVE YOUR LIFE.

How you live your life is determined by your choices. To make those choices good ones, make them consciously and constructively. Life is challenging, but not impossible. Living it effectively takes preparation and planning. Life is full of opportunities. Seizing opportunities requires that you make choices. Learning how to make better choices increases the odds that your life will be meaningful, satisfying and productive.

A. PRACTICE THE GOLDEN RULE

"Do unto others what you would have them do unto you."

This simple, yet immensely powerful, concept has the potential to change lives (especially your own) and to change the world.

Think about how different the world would be if we would all just follow this basic guideline for respecting the value of other lives. There would be no war, no crime no hatred, no class conflict, no social strife. In this simple concept, humankind has literally had for centuries the answer to most of the world's problems, but refuses to recognize and implement that answer.

Many of us acknowledge the wisdom of the message but fail to follow it for a variety of reasons: We are focused on "me" and what's in it for "me". We are distrustful and fearful of those of different skin colors, religions, social class, language, etc. It violates our sense of what is "fair" – "people treat me poorly, why should I be nice to them."; etc. etc. None of which are legitimate reasons for not doing what is admittedly hard work, but the right thing to do.

This is not a new concept, nor, as we Christians like to believe, is it unique to Christianity. We associate it with Jesus's Sermon on the Mount, when in fact the concept was recognized as foundational and critical to human relationships by many cultures hundreds of years before Jesus preached its value. I was interested to find the following examples:

"In everything, do to others what you would have them do to you. Matthew: 7:12, Luke,6:31

"You shall love your neighbor as yourself" Matthew 22:40

"Hurt not others with that which pains yourself" – Buddhism

"Do not impose on others what you yourself do not desire" – Confucius

"This is the sum of duty: do naught to others which if done to thee would cause thee pain. – Hinduism

"No one of you is a believer until he desires for his brother that which he desires for himself. – Islam

"What is hateful to you, do not do to your neighbor." – Judaism/Talmud

"Whatever is disagreeable to yourself do not do unto others." – Zoroastrianism

"Chose thou for thy neighbor that which thou chooseth for thyself." - Baha'i

"One who is going to take a pointed stick to pinch a baby bird should first try it on himself to feel how it hurts." - Nigerian Proverb.

"A man should wander about treating all creatures as he himself would be treated." -Jainism

I particularly like the Nigerian version. Note that the Jainism version extends the courtesy to all "creatures".

If we would but follow the Golden Rule, we would feel good about ourselves and make the world a better place because of our contributions. The Golden Rule has "Golden Possibilities". **PRACTICE IT.** If we were to vow every morning that today we will treat others as we would like to be treated, regardless of how they treat us, our lives would be richer and far less stressful.

B. DEVELOP LIFE GOALS and OBJECTIVES

Defining clear personal goals and objectives keeps us focused on who we want to be and what we want to accomplish. Goal setting is the first step in turning the intangible into the tangible. Our most important goals and objectives are those which define the kind of person we want to be.

> "People with goals succeed because they know where they're going."
>
> Earl Nightingale

Stephen Covey, in The 7 Habits of Highly Effective People, phrases it as: "Begin With the End in Mind", i.e. start with a clear idea of your destination, your goals and objectives. To help us get started, he suggests that we all complete the following exercise:

> "See yourself going to the funeral of a loved one. As you enter the funeral parlor or chapel, you see the faces of friends and family. You feel the shared sorrow of losing someone important, the joy of having known the deceased, which radiates from the hearts of the people

around you. As you walk to the front of the room and look into the casket, you come face to face with yourself. This is your funeral. All of these people have come to honor you, to express feelings of love and appreciation for your life.

The program in your hand indicates that there are to be four speakers, the first from your immediate family, the second a close friend, someone who can relate who you were as a person, the third is an associate with whom you worked for a long time and the fourth is someone from your church or other organization where you were involved in service.

Now think deeply. What would you like for them to have seen in you? What contributions, what achievements would you want them to remember? Look carefully at the people around you. What difference would you have liked to have made in their lives?"

Think carefully about what you want those closest to you to think and say about you. Start right now living a life consistent with the values that will enable, those who care about you, (and especially to enable you), to truthfully understand that you made a positive difference in people's lives.

Goals are statements (decisions) about what you want to accomplish and stand for in your life. Your goals should include statements about the kind of person you want to be (I want to be a good friend), what you want to accomplish (I want to write a book about decision making), and what you want to experience (I want to visit all the US National Parks). Goals are longer term and more general than objectives. Goals should establish the direction and parameters for your life. Goals should incorporate your values. When determining goals, it is useful to test them against your statements of values, and vice versa, to assure that they are consistent. Inconsistencies may warrant modifications to one or the other. That's ok. Inconsistencies aren't.

A worksheet for defining your goals is provided in Appendix F.

Objectives define results to be accomplished in specific, measurable terms, with specified due dates. Always ask: what are the end results that I want? The attainment of objectives provides the building blocks for the accomplishment of goals. Objectives are end results to be achieved within a certain period of time. To be effective determinants of personal effectiveness, goals and objectives must be integrated, i.e. they must be consistent and mutually supportive. The attainment of objectives must lead to the accomplishment of goals, which, in turn, fulfill your personal purpose.

The following are examples of goals and objectives that illustrate the distinction between them:

> Goal: I want to be a good student, to take full advantage of my school opportunities.

> Related Objective: I will turn in all assignments when due.

> Related Objective: I will contribute something in each class at least three times per week.

> Goal: I want to help relieve life's burdens for those less fortunate.

> Related Objective: By the end of this month I will select a social services agency to which I will commit at least six hours of effort every month.

Think about goals and objectives in each area of your life:

- Family
- Physical & Health
- Career
- Spiritual
- Moral & Ethical
- Financial
- Mental & Educational

It is imperative to write down your goals and objectives. Writing forces you to think about and clarify your targets. It also increases the probability of reaching your goals. Various research studies have found that those who write their goals and objectives are from three to nine times as likely to achieve them as those who don't. Whether the most accurate multiplier is three or nine is not important. The fact is that writing them significantly increases the probability of achieving them. **WRITE THEM DOWN!**

> "You control your future, your destiny. What you think about, comes about. By recording your dreams and goals on paper, you set in motion the process of becoming the person you most want to be. Put your future in good hands – your own."
>
> Mark Victor Hansen

Some other guidelines for developing goals and objectives:

- **Personalize** - Assure that your goals are things you really want, not just statements designed to impress someone. Goals are personal. Make them yours.
- **Be Specific** - Make your goal and objective statements definitive. Identify exactly what you want in as much detail as possible.

- **Be Realistic** – Goals and objectives should be <u>attainable</u>. They should require stretch but be achievable. The right amount of stretch is a tough call. You should be looking for the right balance of challenge and reason. Many err on the side of aiming too low. We tend to underestimate our potentials. However, consistently missing unrealistically high targets can frustrate and discourage. Construct some goals you are reasonably certain of attaining. Success builds confidence and confidence generates more success.

- **Measure** - Find a way to make goals and objectives <u>measurable.</u> Not all will be quantifiable. Use numbers if you can, but if numbers don't fit, find another yardstick. It's hard to put a number on attaining a specific diploma, degree, certificate or license, but when you hold the document with your name on it in your hand; you know you've accomplished something. Measurements are important for indicating when you've hit your target, and equally important, for indicating progress. Use measurements to determine if you are really spending time on the things you have identified as important.

- **Use Benchmarks** - For long term goals, establish benchmarks, (shorter term targets), to measure progress.

- **Be Positive** - Write goal and objective statements in the positive rather than the negative. Use positive words like "achieve", "become" and "obtain" instead of "avoid" "reduce" or "less". Instead of declaring that you want to reduce the time you spend watching TV, state that you intend to read at least 18 thought provoking books per year. Instead of saying "I want to lose 13 pounds", say "I want to achieve a weight of 175 lbs. and be able to run a mile in 8 minutes by May 31".

- **Be Consistent** - Assure that your goals are not conflicting or mutually exclusive. Test them against each other. If your goal is to be a social worker, it is not likely that you can realistically expect to live in an 18 room mansion with an ocean view, (unless you have another source of wealth).

- **Set Dates** -Your targets should be time specific. Goals are typically long term and include what you want to be, so target dates can be more nebulous. Objectives should each have a clear target date for attainment.

- **Focus** – Attainment is significantly dependent upon focused attention and effort. Problems with achievement can often be traced to lack of focus. Few of us can effectively pursue fifteen objectives simultaneously. Prioritize and then stagger target dates to assure that attainment is realistic. Then really concentrate on a few high priorities.

- **Share Selectively** – Share them with one or a few persons whose advice you trust, and ask those persons to periodically review progress with you and hold you accountable.

- **Review** – Keep goal and objective statements visible and review them periodically, (at least once every three months). For maximum effectiveness, internalize them to the extent that they are a part of your consciousness for automatic reference when making serious decisions.

The most important <u>benefit</u> of setting and writing down goals doesn't come from the attainment of the goals, but from the self–awareness, discipline and priorities established by going through the <u>process</u>. Taking goal and objective setting seriously can make a positive difference in your life, and testing your decisions against your goals and objectives can help you make significantly better decisions.

Aim high when selecting goals but consider not only the results you want but also the price you are willing to pay to achieve those results. Realistically assess the effort, sacrifices and the tradeoffs necessary to realize a particular dream. High personal costs should not automatically dissuade you from pursuing a goal. Just be sure you understand the price and are willing to pay it.

> "When we are motivated by goals that have deep
> meaning, by dreams that need completion, by pure love
> that needs expressing, then we truly live."

> Greg Anderson

Developing goals and objectives is important to the accomplishment of any endeavor, but merely developing them is not the end. Having established goals and objectives, it is imperative to ask: what do I have to know and learn to achieve them? How do I learn what I need to know? What do I have to do to achieve them? Without the required knowledge and a plan of action, goals become wishes with little chance of realization.

When making important decisions, always consider whether a course of action enhances or impedes your ability to achieve your goals and objectives.

You can define your objectives on the worksheet in Appendix G.

C. THINK POSITIVELY

I received the following as an email from an associate. It illustrates the importance of attitude choices. I thought it worth sharing.

> *"John is the kind of guy you love to hate. He is always in a*
> *good mood and always has something positive to*
> *say. When someone would ask him how he was doing, he*

55

would reply, 'If I were any better, I would be twins!"

He was a natural motivator.
If an employee was having a bad day, John was there telling the employee how to look on the positive side of the situation.

Seeing this style really made me curious, so one day I went up and asked him, 'I don't get it!' 'You can't be a positive person all of the time. How do you do it?'

He replied, 'Each morning I wake up and say to myself, you have two choices today. You can choose to be in a good mood or...you can choose to be in a bad mood. I choose to be in a good mood. Each time something bad happens, I can choose to be a victim or...I can choose to learn from it. I choose to learn from it.

Every time someone comes to me complaining, I can choose to accept their complaining or....I can point out the positive side of life. I choose the positive side of life.

'Yeah, right, it's not that easy,' I protested.

'Yes, it is,' he said. 'Life is all about choices. When you cut away all the junk, every situation is a choice. You choose how you react to situations. You choose how people affect your mood.

You choose to be in a good mood or bad mood. The bottom line: It's your choice how you live your life.

I reflected on what he said. Soon thereafter, I left the Tower Industry to start my own business. We lost touch, but I often thought about him when I made a choice about life, instead of reacting to it.

Several years later, I heard that he was involved in a serious accident, falling some 60 feet from a communications tower.

After 18 hours of surgery and weeks of intensive care, he was released from the hospital with rods placed in his back.

I saw him about six months after the accident.

When I asked him how he was, he replied, 'If I were any better, I'd be twins...wanna see my scars?'

I declined to see his wounds, but I did ask him what had gone through his mind as the accident took place.

'The first thing that went through my mind was the well-being of my soon-to-be born daughter,' he replied. 'Then, as I lay on the ground, I remembered that I had two choices: I could choose to live or...I could choose to die. I chose to live.'

'Weren't you scared? Did you lose consciousness?' I asked.

He continued, '....the paramedics were great. They kept telling me I was going to be fine. But when they wheeled me into the ER and I saw the expressions on the faces of the doctors and nurses, I got really scared. In their eyes, I read 'he's a dead man'. I knew I needed to take action. 'What did you do?' I asked.

'Well, there was a big burly nurse shouting questions at me,' said John. 'She asked if I was allergic to anything 'Yes, I replied..' The doctors and nurses stopped working as they waited for my reply.. I took a deep breath and yelled, Gravity'.

Over their laughter, I told them, 'I am choosing to live. Operate on me as if I am alive, not dead.'

He lived, thanks to the skill of his doctors, but also because of his amazing attitude...I learned from him that every day we have the choice to live fully.

Attitude, after all, is everything."

Attitude is a choice. A positive attitude increases the probabilities that outcomes will be positive. Think positively! Do not let what you can't do prevent you from doing what you can do.

D. SERVE – DETERMINE HOW YOU WILL "GIVE BACK"

Life itself is a gift we did nothing to "earn". In addition, no one makes it through life entirely on his or her own merits. We all owe others. Life is a blessing we should acknowledge by contributing to the lives of others. We can take nothing with us from this life, but we can and should leave behind us something worthwhile. Living a meaningful life means making the world a better place because we lived.

> *"Life's most persistent and urgent question is: What are you doing for others?"*
>
> Dr. Martin Luther King Jr

Giving back is a win-win proposition. By serving, we not only improve the lives of others, but also reap personal benefits. A Harvard Business School study confirmed that: "happier people give more and giving makes people happier, such that happiness and giving may operate in a positive feedback loop." Those who receive help are grateful for the help and volunteers learn that helping others makes them feel better. Unlike giving money, giving time, energy and effort directly, provides immediate feedback about what your contribution means to those receiving it. Our lives are richer, more full and complete through attending to the healing of others.

Giving generates hope. We can each be part of the problem or part of the solution.

> *"There is a light in the world, a healing spirit more powerful than any darkness we may encounter. We sometimes lose sight of this force when there is suffering, too much pain. Then suddenly, the spirit will emerge through the lives of ordinary people who hear a call and answer in extraordinary ways."*
>
> Mother Teresa

Choose to be one of those who hears and answers. We each have something to offer. Giving should not be driven by feelings of guilt or obligation, but an expression of gratitude that we have the ability, and a response to the understanding that we are all interrelated and interdependent.

> *"An individual has not started living until he can rise above the narrow confines of his individualistic concerns to the broader concerns of all humanity."*
>
> Martin Luther King, Jr.

A defining factor in living a meaningful life is contributing to something above and beyond self. We should consciously choose to invest time where our efforts will yield a return for others. Gifts do not have to be costly. The gift of friendship or simply one's presence can make a difference in a life.

When selecting an area in which to give back, it is important to select a cause in which one has an interest and abilities. That makes it more fun. Do something. Make a commitment. It is better if it represents an on-going commitment rather than a one-time shot. Finding a way to help people help themselves can be particularly rewarding.

In Appendix H, is a list of several ways one can give back. It is by no means exhaustive. Think of some others you can add in the spaces. For more ideas, take a look at
www.volunteermatch.org.

In the final analysis, all we really own is our lives. It is how we use our lives that determine what kind of people we are. As Mother Teresa observed, we don't have to do great things, only lots of small things with great love. It is by serving and giving that we find life.

E. PRACTICE COMPASSION

Demonstrating compassion, the sharing of someone's pain, discomfort, dilemma, loss or unfortunate circumstance, is the "right" thing to do. To care enough to take on some of the burden, so that another person does not have to bear problems alone, can be extremely helpful and meaningful, to both the recipient and the giver.

> "To give pleasure to a single heart by a single act is
> better than a thousand heads bowing in prayer."
>
> Mahatma Gandhi

Understanding and demonstrating compassion may be critical to the very survival of humankind and the world we share with other creatures. The root of the word is the Latin "compati" which means "to suffer with". But the concept involves more than pity. It involves: (1) being aware of the suffering of others, (2) feeling empathy for the one suffering, and (3) taking action to alleviate that suffering.

> "It is one of the most beautiful compensations of this life that no man can sincerely help another without helping himself."
>
> Ralph Waldo Emerson

F. BE GENEROUS.

Generosity is rooted in the belief that we receive many gifts and thus have the obligation and privilege to "give back". Giving to another enhances the development of relationships, and reinforces the perception that a "good" person is one who shares.

> "There is a wonderful, almost mystical law of nature that says three of the things we want most – happiness, freedom, and peace of mind – are always attained when we give them to others."
>
> John Wooden.

G. BE GRATEFUL.

We sometimes are so obsessed with what we want that we fail to appreciate what we have. We are all blessed in multiple ways and have much for which we should be grateful. Feeling and expressing appreciation for those blessings is a basic obligation. An appropriate principle is to expect nothing and appreciate the value of everything. Gratitude is more than an obligation. Studies show that it has personal benefits for the one demonstrating it. Sonja Lyubomirsky, in her book *The How of Happiness*, writes:

> "People who are consistently grateful have been found to be relatively happier, more energetic, and more hopeful and to report experiencing more frequent positive emotions. They also tend to be more helpful and empathic, more spiritual and religious, more forgiving, and less materialistic than others who are less predisposed to gratefulness. Furthermore, the more a person is inclined to gratitude, the less likely he or she is to be depressed, anxious, lonely, envious or neurotic."

Feeling and expressing gratitude is not only the right thing to do, it has positive personal rewards.

A Point to Ponder: Consider making a list of all the people for whom you are thankful. Then write a note to one of them telling them why you are thankful that they are a part of your life.

H. ACCEPT RESPONSIBILITY.

No matter how good or bad your decisions, you are responsible for the consequences. You are responsible for your thoughts, beliefs, values, words, choices and actions. You are responsible for how you treat other people, for keeping your promises, for your life and personal well-being. Blaming others or finding excuses does not change that reality. Recognizing and accepting this responsibility will motivate you to make better decisions.

Being responsible requires self-discipline and effective time management. It means being conscientious, mindful, accountable and dependable. Be particularly conscious of what you say, for words can wound deeper than a knife. Accept that you have control. If you don't do <u>something</u>, nothing is going to get better. Choose not to be a victim. Don't, as many do, blame your circumstances on someone else's actions or on the "system". Accepting responsibility is the first step to finding solutions.

Don't fall into the trap of blaming someone or circumstances for your actions, as in: "I wouldn't have done that if she hadn't ….., or "he (or the devil) <u>made</u> me do it." Don't offer lame excuses: "I felt hurt, so I …", "I felt angry, so I ….", "I felt afraid, so I …". "I couldn't help it." You have a choice about how you respond to circumstances and the actions of others. You are responsible for your feelings and your actions.

Be pro-active. Avoid the mindset of "Why doesn't someone do something?" Instead ask "What should I do?" Then do something.

Forego any feelings of entitlement. A journalist for *TIME* characterized this "entitlement" attitude of far too many as follows: "If I want it, I need it. If I need it, I have a right to it. If I have a right to it, someone owes it to me...". The concept of accepting responsibility is contrary to the idea of entitlement. Accept responsibility.

The respect and trust of persons who you respect, and trust are valuable assets. You earn that respect and trust by being competent and accountable and by accepting responsibility for your actions.

Take responsibility for learning to make better decisions. Make the best decision you know how to make and take responsibility for the consequences.

I. MAINTAIN SELF CONTROL

Demonstrating self-control involves choosing thoughtful, rational responses to stimuli which are consistent with one's values and goals. It is the process of avoiding compulsive, self-destructive reactions to temptations, threats, addictions or provocations. Permitting negative emotions to influence decisions can have devastating effects. Self-control is about being the master of one's life rather than the slave to one's emotions. It is not about taking all the fun out of life. It is about making intelligent choices. Self-control is a combination of will, commitment, courage and taking responsibility for one's actions. It is also a concept of free will and choice. You have to choose to exercise it.

> "If you are not in control of your thoughts, then you are not in control of yourself. Without self-control, you have no real power, regardless of whatever else you accomplish. If you are not aware of the thoughts that you are thinking, then you are a rider with no reins, with no power over where you are going. You cannot control what you are not aware of. Awareness must come first."
>
> Thomas M. Steiner

Developing self-control involves awareness, the understanding that we can choose our emotions and thoughts, and the identification of our personal "hot buttons", those stimuli that typically set off "automatic, personal and/or relationship damaging, emotional responses.

To establish control:

1. Identify personal issues/instances over which you wish to exert more effective control.

2. Identify the damaging, typical reactions to which you are prone and the emotions that drive them.
3. Make a decision to develop more effective responses.
4. Tell yourself: "I am in control of my thoughts, emotions and reactions, I am in charge of my behavior".
5. Visualize how you would like to calmly and rationally deal with the issue.
6. Recognize the volatile issue when they come up and practice your planned responses.

The good news is that, like a muscle, self-control gets stronger with regular exercise. The important thing is to practice overriding damaging, habitual ways of doing things and exerting deliberate control over your actions.

> "Never respond to an angry person with a fiery comeback, even if he deserves it. Don't allow his anger to become your anger."

> Bohdi Sanders

We can control our thoughts. That's a powerful concept that can make a difference in life. Practice it.

J. SEEK & PRESERVE BEAUTY

There is beauty all around us, but we often miss it. We are naturally drawn to beauty, but get distracted by "entertainment" and mental clutter. Beauty can be seen, heard, sensed or felt. Beauty is something that generates in us a feeling of pleasure. Roses, sunsets, mountains, good music, the face of a sleeping baby, are all beautiful, but so also are acts of compassion and kindness. Beauty is physical, emotional and spiritual.

> "Begin with the beautiful, and it leads you to the true."

> Father Robert Barron

65

Beauty satisfies us, comforts us, inspires us, adds meaning to our lives. Recognizing and adding to the beauty in the world is both an obligation and a blessing.

> "Let the beauty that we love be what we do."
>
> Rumi

Walk alone and listen to the beautiful messages of the birds, the flowers, the trees, the clouds, your own mind. Be sensitive to the beauty that lies in acts of love. Don't let the beauty of the world and life escape you.

Beauty:

> Look for it.
> Appreciate it.
> Enhance it.
> Restore it.
> Create it.
> Live it.

K. SEEK BALANCE & HARMONY.

Making wise choices requires our best efforts and we can expect those best efforts only if our lives are in "balance" and "harmony". Humans do not perform at their best when torn by inner conflicts.

Internal conflicts are often the cause of conflicts with others. When we are stressed, we tend to be impatient, short and disagreeable with others, especially those important in our lives. These confrontations lead to further inner turmoil and we become involved in a vicious cycle which impedes effective decision making.

> "Happiness is not a matter of intensity but of balance, order, rhythm and harmony."
>
> Thomas Merton

Finding balance and harmony in our lives is not easy. Life is full of struggles to find the correct balance between conflicting demands, aspirations and priorities. Finding and adhering to the "right" balance between family and work, work and play, self-interest and the welfare of others, things material and things spiritual, all involve important decisions. Deciding how good is "good enough" is another perplexing issue. I strongly support a commitment to doing "well" anything worth doing and have little patience with shoddy workmanship, yet I understand that it is not practical or necessary.to do everything perfectly. We have to choose carefully which issues warrant any effort at all, and how much effort to expend on each.

Who we are is determined by our choices about the way we see things and how we respond to what happens around us and within us. We maintain harmony in relationships: by recognizing and respecting the rights of others to make their own decisions, by avoiding attempts to impose our will on others in an attempt to exercise personal power, allay our fears or "prove the superiority" of our beliefs. Disharmony means our energies are unfocused or poorly focused.

Living in harmony means being in step with the universe, with reality. It means recognizing the intricate interdependence of all things. It means seeking what is "true". It means feeling at peace with what "is". It means being connected to the earth and all living things.

> "A lot of the conflict you have in your life exists simply because you're not living in alignment; you're not being true to yourself."
>
> Steve Maraboli,

An important part of balance is being aware of, and genuinely thankful for, all the many wonderful things we receive, both from nature and from other people, and in turn, attempting to *give* as much as we *receive*. Balance also involves taking into account what we *feel* as well as what we *know*, what we *believe* as well as what we *experience*. Understanding balance and harmony involves understanding that choices and actions have consequences.

- One creates harmony or disharmony by the life choices one makes.
- Harmony is achieved by a careful balancing of: self-awareness, life purpose and inner strength, a sense of belonging, personal ability, self-discipline and generosity.
- Being in control of one's emotions is critical to achieving harmony.
- We all need something to believe in, someone to love, something worthwhile to do and something to look forward to.
- Internal harmony and balance involve being at peace with (and not abusing) one's body, thoughts and emotions. Holding a grudge or coveting a neighbor's possessions creates disruptions to harmony.
- Being out of harmony can cause physical and psychological illnesses. Getting oneself back into a state of harmony should be a constant priority.
- Social harmony is necessary among people to enable them to work and live together effectively.
- Spiritual harmony should be nurtured between human beings and the spiritual world through respect, prayer and living a "good" life.
- Natural harmony is valued as necessary for peaceful coexistence between human beings and the natural world of animals, plants and all the natural elements that surround us.

"Always aim at complete harmony of thought
and word and deed. Always aim at purifying
your thoughts and everything will be well."

Mahatma Gandhi

We should strive to live in harmony with people and with nature. The concept includes principles for guiding one's thoughts, speech, actions and behavior. These principles represent a worldview and a philosophy, a comprehensive and complex network of ideas, encompassing both a way of living and a state of being.

The concept recognizes that individuals have the ability to choose: to positively control their lives through responsible thought, speech and behavior, or to destroy their lives and negatively impact the lives of others by thinking, speaking and behaving irresponsibly. It emphasizes accepting personal responsibility for one's actions and regularly taking corrective measures to maintain, and/or return to, balance and harmony. Looking for the beauty and lessons in every human experience helps one maintain inner harmony. The philosophy identifies key elements of moral and ethical behavior and important relationship principles necessary for living a long, harmonious and meaningful life.

The concept encompasses: the meanings of the words: beauty, goodness, well-being, harmony, happiness, completeness, perfection and order. It means living the "right way. It means seeking harmony and balance within one's self, with other persons, with all living things and with one's natural environment. It includes seeking and respecting the beauty in all things.

Living in right relationships requires that one be aware and receptive, recognizing that everything that happens to us has a message for us, something for us to learn. We need to "listen" for, and be receptive to, these messages. Reflecting on both positive and negative experiences, we should ask ourselves:

- What is this experience teaching me about myself, about others and about living?
- What am I teaching others through the way that I live?

Michael Garrett, *WRITTEN ON THE WIND*

Choosing Balance and Harmony - Finding balance and harmony depends upon making the right choices. Making the right choices often depends on asking the right questions. Seeking and understanding basic truths helps one make the right choices.

> "Well-being occurs when we seek and find our unique place in the universe and experience the continuous cycle of receiving and giving through respect and reverence for the beauty of all living things. Stated another way, everyone and everything was created with a specific purpose to fulfill, and no one should have the power to interfere or impose on others the best path to follow."

Michael Garrett, *WALKING ON THE WIND,*

Finding the right balance and harmony takes conscious effort. We need first to achieve internal harmony. The mind, the heart and the body must be in harmony. Harmony can best be approached by; carefully selecting a set of values and principles, living a life consistent with those values and principles, being thankful, giving back and by listening to the guidance and wisdom of one's inner voice. We realize our lives are in balance and we find peace of mind and satisfaction when our values, principles goals, attention and behavior are all in alignment.

70

L. DEMONSTRATE RESPECT AND REVERENCE FOR NATURE

It is critical that we understand that our relationship with Nature, and the relationship of the elements of nature to each other, are all interdependent. Animals feed on plants and in turn animals are food for each other and for humans. Humankind exhales carbon dioxide and inhales oxygen. Trees exhale oxygen and inhale carbon dioxide. We have an obligation of reciprocity, that when we take something from Nature we should give something back, to maintain the crucial balance. We have a real and necessary responsibility for the guardianship of nature. The earth is not just a repository of natural resources to be exploited, it is a manifestation of life.

"The Nature vision, the gift of seeing truly, with wonder and delight into the natural world, is informed by a certain attitude of reverence and respect. It is a matter of extrasensory as well as sensory perception. In addition to the eye, it involves the intelligence, the instinct and the imagination. It is the perception not only of objects and forms but also of essences and ideals."

N. Scott Momaday – Kiowa

Modern environmental problems have become so serious that they constitute a global crisis. We are fouling our nest. Native Americans lived comfortably with nature for thousands of years. Conservation was a basic value of their culture. White cultures strive to <u>control</u> nature. The Indigenous People focused on <u>cooperating</u> with nature. We should do likewise.

Nature should be honored as the source of the plants, animals and water that sustain our lives. More than that, we must see ourselves as part of nature, not as some higher species empowered with the privilege of exploiting nature. We should not see ourselves as having "dominion" over nature, but as a part of nature, with respect and stewardship for all other parts. We should understand that humans are not above nature, but that humans require nature to make humans "whole".

Any desecration of nature, or taking from nature more than one requires, should be viewed as stealing from one's children and grandchildren, all future generations.

> "Treat the earth well: it was not given to you by your parents, it was loaned to you by your children. We do not inherit the Earth from our ancestors, we borrow it from our children."
>
> Ancient Native American Proverb

> "Every human being has a sacred duty to protect the welfare of Mother Earth, from whom all life comes. In order to do this, we must recognize the enemy...the one within us. We must begin with ourselves."
>
> Leon Shenandoah – Onadaga Chief

Human-kind's responsibilities to Nature include:

- Continually giving thanks for the life-giving power of the sun, for the earth and the water and food the earth provides.
- Never taking more than one needs.
- Giving thanks for what we do take.
- Replenishing what is taken.
- Doing as little damage as possible.
- Taking time to appreciate the beauty of the earth.

> "The lands of the planet call to human-kind for redemption. But it is a redemption of sanity, not a supernatural reclamation project at the end of history. The planet itself calls to the other living species for

relief. Religion cannot be kept within the bounds of sermons and scriptures. It is a force in and of itself and calls for the integration of lands and peoples in harmonious unity. The land waits for those who can discern its rhythms. ... and for relief from the constant burden of exploitation."

Vine Deloria Jr. *GOD IS RED*

Too many people just don't "get it".

"When you have pollution in one place, it spreads all over, just as arthritis or cancer spreads in the body. The earth is sick now because the earth is being mistreated. It is very important for people to understand this. The earth is a living organism which has a will and wants to be well. Too many people don't know that when they harm the earth, they harm themselves and when they harm themselves, they harm the earth."

Rolling Thunder - Cherokee

In *VOICES IN THE STONES*, Kent Nerburn quotes a Native American elder who said:

"Nature has rules. Nature has laws. You think that you can ignore the rules or, if you don't like them, you can change them. But Mother Earth doesn't change the rules. When you can count the animals, you're getting near the end of your chances. We can count the eagles. We can count the buffalo. I've heard that in India and Africa they can count the tigers and the elephants. That's Mother Earth crying out. She's giving us a warning and She's begging for her life. And here's what your people don't ever seem to learn. There's going to become a day when things can't be fixed. And you know what? It's going to be a day just like today."

Nature as Teacher - Nature is a vast reservoir of knowledge to be tapped by observation and experience. Humans are not distinct from nature, but a part of nature. Every animal, every plant, every natural event has a lesson to convey. Observe how animals and birds care for their families. Observe what a tree limb's reaction to the wind has to teach us about the need for flexibility in our lives. By understanding nature, we can better understand ourselves. Humankind's role is to discover the rules of the universe and to learn to live in a right relationship with them. Everything that happens has a message, something to be learned. To learn from nature involves the use of all our senses. It requires that we become involved with nature and that we become constantly observant and aware. Nature has much to teach us, if we will but open our minds.

> "It remains for us to learn once again that we are a part of nature, not a transcendent species with no responsibilities to the natural world."

> Vine Deloria, *GOD IS RED*

Indigenous People found meaning in their relationship to, and love for, Mother Earth and her creatures. If we care, observe and listen, we can do likewise.

M. USE TIME WISELY

Time is our most precious resource. Time decisions are among the most important we make. We make decisions all day, every day, about how we are going to use our time. We may ask ourselves: "what am I going to do: today? this morning? for the next hour?, for the next ten minutes?", or we may not consciously ask these critical questions and just let time slide. Remember that a decision not to decide is still a decision. How you answer these questions affects the quality of your life. When you are asked to do something, or decide to do something, that requires a commitment of your time,

74

understand that the commitment is for a piece of your life. Recognize that your time = your life. Ask yourself if playing time-devouring video games or watching mind-numbing TV is really how you want to spend your <u>life</u>.

> "Dost thou love life? Then do not squander time, for that's the stuff life is made of."

> Benjamin Franklin.

Priorities shape our choices. Among the most frequent decisions we make, ones to which we typically give little thought, and the decisions that have a huge impact on our lives, are decisions about how we spend our time. In <u>THE SEVEN HABITS OF HIGHLY EFFECTICE PEOPLE</u>, Stephen Covey talks about "Putting First Things First". What he means is: work on the most important things, the things that will have the greatest impact, that make a difference, before spending time on trivial things. When deciding what to do next, we often opt for what gives us the most immediate satisfaction, or the easiest, or the most nagging project, rather than the one which will yield the most benefits.

> "Most of us spend too much time on what is urgent and not enough time on what is important."

> Stephen R. Covey

Covey suggests that we each ask ourselves this basic question: "What one thing could I do (that I'm not doing now) that if I did it on a regular basis would make a tremendous difference in my personal life?" Identify that one thing, make doing it a priority. Do it.

Effective activity management involves defining a valid set of values, goals and objectives and then comparing the relative worth of activities based on their consistency with those standards. There is a huge difference between urgency and importance. We should manage our time and our lives around importance.

Covey developed a model for categorizing and managing activities:

TIME MANAGEMENT MATRIX

	Urgent	Not Urgent
I m p o r t a n t	I ACTIVITIES Crises Pressing Problems Deadline -driven projects	II ACTIVITIES Planning Prevention Relationship Building Identifying New Opportunities Recreation Skill Building Preparing
N o t I m p o r t a n t	III Interruptions Junk Mail Some meetings Near Term Pressing Deadlines Popular Activities	IV Trivia, Busy Work Junk emails Trivial Phone Calls Time Wasters Chit Chat Video games

Figure 1

There are always urgent and important activities that must be done (Quadrant I) but most of us spend an amazing portion of our time doing what is not important (Quadrants III and IV). We spend far too little time on Quadrant II activities because they are not urgent and sometimes require more effort. Yet these are the most productive activities. Quadrant II activities produce results and reduce the number of Quadrant I crises.

A Point to Ponder: Estimate what percentage of your time you spend in each of the above quadrants.

Our actions express our priorities. What we do matters so much more than what we intended to do. We must determine our priorities and then conduct our lives in accordance with them.

> "Things which matter most must never be at the mercy of things which matter least."

> Johann Wolfgang von Goethe

The key is not just to prioritize your "to do list", but to first be sure the right things are on your to do list (including Quadrant II, the important but not urgent, activities), and then act on them.

> "The life you have left is a gift. Cherish it. Enjoy it now, to the fullest. Do what matters, now."

> Leo Babauta

When thinking about time, think not about saving time, but "Making Time" for things that matter. Make a list of the distractions, (junk emails, social media, videos, etc.) that steal your time every day. Identify ways to eliminate those thieves from your agenda. At the end of each day, or the first thing in the morning, select two or three significant tasks for the day. Write them down. Schedule one or more times to work on those tasks. Lock out the distractions. Focus during those times. Get the tasks done.

This is not to imply that we should work all the time. Everyone needs to spend time having fun, learning, exercising, spiritually recharging and just relaxing. Just be conscious of the importance of time and intentional about how you use it.

Time is almost always an important element of decision making. We often do not have the time to gather and analyze all the information we would like before a decision must be made. How you use the time that is available is important.

When framing the issue that requires a decision, identify the time when you want to make your choice, and schedule backwards from there, so that you can give the decision the time and effort you decide it warrants.

Don't procrastinate! The bane of effective decision making is putting off working at the issue until there is insufficient time for careful analysis and reflection, and/or some good options are no longer available. Hasty decisions about important issues are often lousy decisions. Take control of the process. Start early and give yourself enough time to do it right.

> "This time, like all times, is a very good one, if we but know how to use it."
>
> Ralph Waldo Emerson

N. LIVE EVERY DAY

Making decisions about how you want to live your life and then consciously living those decisions makes life fulfilling and meaningful. Pope John XXIII elaborated on this focus in a treatise entitled JUST FOR TODAY:

"Just for today,
I will try to live for this day alone,
Without wishing to solve my life's problems all at once.

Just for today,
I will take care of how I present myself: I will dress
simply; I will not raise my voice.
I will be polite in my manners; I will not criticize anyone;
I will not look to improve or discipline anyone other than
myself.

Just for today,
I will be happy in the certainty that I was created to be

happy,
not only in the world to come, but also in this one

Just for today,
I will adapt to circumstances, without expecting
circumstances to adapt to my wishes.

Just for today,
I will devote ten minutes of my time to sitting in silence
and listening to God,
remembering that, just as food is necessary for the life of
the body,
so silence and listening are necessary for the life of the
soul.

Just for today,
I will do a good deed and tell no one about it.

Just for today,
I will do at least one thing that I do not enjoy, and if my
feelings are hurt,
I will make sure no one notices.

Just for today,
I will make a plan: perhaps I will not follow it perfectly, but
still I will make it.
And I will guard against two obstacles, haste and
indecision.

Just for today,
I will know from the bottom of my heart, no matter how it
will seem,
that God cares for me like no one else in this world.

Just for today,
I will have no fears. In particular, I will not be afraid
to enjoy what is beautiful and to believe in love.

*I can easily do for twelve hours, what I would find
daunting if I had to do for a lifetime."*

*Not bad guidelines by which to live our lives - just for
today!*

O. RELISH EXPERIENCES.

Seek out and learn from experiences. Experiences open our eyes to truth and understanding. Education is not just about learning facts. Education is about participating in life and learning as one participates. Involvement is key to understanding. Observe, listen and reflect. Every choice, every action has consequences. Examine them to unlock the lessons to be learned.

Make a list of the seven to ten most significant experiences of your life to date. Then note what lessons you learned from each. Consider both positive and negative lessons. Think about how you can apply those lessons to future decisions and circumstances.

A Point to Ponder: Think about an interest you have that could be explored by a future experience. Plan it. Do it.

P. PRACTICE MINDFULNESS

There are two elements to mindfulness: being <u>aware</u>, being conscious of what is present, and what is going on around us, and having the ability to <u>concentrate</u>, to focus on one thing, to give that one thing our undivided attention so we can deal with it most effectively.

> *"The mind is just like a muscle – the more you exercise
> it, the stronger it gets and the more it can expand."*
>
> Idowu Koyenikan

Awareness. You have probably observed people who seemed oblivious to what was going on around them, who were out of touch with reality. This "condition" is hardly conducive to making good choices. Circumstances matter, conditions matter, context matters, how the world really works (reality) matters. Being aware means being conscious of everything that affects our: interests, actions, goals, objectives and values. Being aware means being willing to confront reality, whether pleasant or unpleasant. Being aware means being conscious of, and respectful of, facts, reality and truth. To learn to make better decisions, we need to learn to be aware.

Awareness is a choice, and also a skill that can be developed. Awareness means being awake to the here and now. It is about being keenly observant of what is going on and why, of what is so, and why.

Be aware that we control awareness like a dimmer switch on an electric light. We can willfully increase or decrease our sensitivity to our surroundings and what is going on. It is not practical to be 100% aware, 100% of the time. Your level of awareness is a choice. Context, the nature and importance of what is present and what is going on should determine where we set our "awareness switch". To operate effectively, we need to determine which things can be left on "automatic", and which things warrant our full attention.

> "Mindfulness means being awake. It means knowing what you are doing."

Jon Kabat-Zinn

Mindfulness means "feeling" life as it happens around us and within us. When mindful, we see things we have not seen before and see things differently than we have seen them before.

Unfortunately, many of us make important, sometimes life changing, decisions with little or no awareness of how those choices will change the shape and direction of our lives. We commit to actions without considering the consequences. Awareness is critical to effective decision making.

One of the characteristics of living mindfully is seeking to understand the reasons for our beliefs. Our actions are driven by our perceptions, of which we may or may not be aware. We need to consciously determine our ideas and values about: what is really important in life, how people should relate to one another, what is right and what is wrong, what is good and what is evil, what constitutes justice and what gives meaning to life. We need to critically examine our perceptions and ensure that they are really ours, not borrowed unconsciously from others.

Mindfulness is our basic tool for adapting to, and successfully coping with, reality.

Focus Our minds naturally have a tendency to jump around from one subject to another like a monkey jumping from one branch to the next. Controlling what Buddhists refer to as our "Monkey Minds", is essential to rational thought and effective decision making. To "bind the monkey" we must understand our minds, our feelings and perceptions and learn to focus on one thing at a time.

> *"Concentration is a cornerstone of mindfulness practice. Your mindfulness will only be as robust as the capacity of your mind to be calm and stable. Without calmness, the mirror of mindfulness will have an agitated and choppy surface and will not be able to reflect things with any accuracy."*
>
> Jon Kabat-Zinn

Increase Mindfulness Fortunately, we can learn to be mindful. Like any life skill, it takes time and effort. The first, and essential, step is to decide that you <u>want</u> to learn to be mindful.

To make better decisions, to make changes, to make improvements, the starting point is awareness. Pay attention. Be "present". When walking a path in the woods, notice the leaves, the weeds, the bark on the trees, the wildlife, the patterns created by sunlight sifting through the canopy. When walking a city street, notice the varying architecture of buildings, the cars passing, and especially the people. When participating in a meeting, observe: not only the content, but the ongoing "process". What does the body language of participants indicate? What role is authority playing in the meeting? What "hidden agendas" are being served? Be observant.

When dealing with a problem or issue, concentrate on concentrating. When your mind strays, gently bring it back to the subject at hand. Focus on your written definition of the issue. It will help you concentrate. Jot down your thoughts. It will help you concentrate.

The "Law of Cause and Effect" asserts that for every effect there is a cause. When you observe an effect, think about, identify, the possible causes.

Many practitioners, myself included, contend that you can train your mind to be more mindful through the practice of meditation. Thich Nhat Hanh defines mindfulness as "keeping one's consciousness alive to the present reality". He contends that meditation that focuses on one's breathing is a useful process for training the mind to be mindful, to become more aware and to increase the ability to focus. When we practice mindfulness in order to build up concentration, mindfulness is like a seed. Properly tended, it grows. Mindfulness frees us of forgetfulness and dispersion and makes it possible to live fully each moment of life. Hanh suggests that "Whenever your mind becomes scattered, use concentrating on your breathing as the means to take hold of your mind again."

To learn more about improving mindfulness through meditation, read *THE MIRACLE OF MINDFULLNESS* by Thich Nhat Hanh.

> *"Training your mind to be in the present moment is the #1 key to making healthier choices."*

> Susan Albers

Q. SELECT A VOCATION.

Choose a vocation carefully. One of the most critical life decisions we make is the choice of the kind of work we do. Work helps define who we are, because that is where we spend a lot of our time. Most of us spend a third or more of our waking hours at some type of occupation, and many spend far more time thinking or worrying about that activity. The wrong choice can lead to what Thoreau described as a life of "quiet desperation". In some cases, the desperation can become more than "quiet".

Choose a vocation, not a job. The word vocation comes from the Latin word for "calling". Our lives will be more pleasant if we can work at something we feel "called" to do. Consciously search for a vocation that interests you, appeals to you, and one from which you can derive satisfaction, not just a living. Research jobs to learn what is actually involved.

First, know yourself. Understand your abilities, interests, and what you don't like. There are multiple "tests" available that

84

attempt to match personal interests and abilities to vocations. Try them.

When considering what you want to do for the remainder of your working life, the following process may prove useful:

- List your strengths and weaknesses
- List your likes and don't likes
- List your vocational goals and ambitions.
- Select the income level you would like to achieve at various points in your career.
- Make a list of the occupations the fit with your self-assessment.
- Gather information about those occupations
- Narrow your list to the few that most interest you.
- Conduct further research. Talk to people in those occupations. Identify the educational and other requirements. Create opportunities to actually try the work to see if it fits.
- Check the alternatives against your values, goals and objectives.
- Make a choice.
- Develop a plan to make your choice happen.

Look for an opportunity to work hard at something worth doing and something you enjoy doing. The benefit of the right vocation is not how much it pays, but what you become.

Make sure that your choice is yours, not what someone thinks you should do or what is available or convenient. If your choice does not work out, don't be afraid to change. Repeat the process and try something else.

R. FACE UP TO ADVERSITY

Ignoring or running away from problems only leads to more problems. The way to fix problems, whether they are the results of your choices or the choices of others, is to make new and better choices. You can't escape life or yourself. Deal with it.

PART V.

CHOOSING WHAT TO EXCLUDE FROM YOUR LIFE.

Some of the most important decisions you make about how to live your life are your choices about what you will exclude from your life. What you <u>don't</u> need in your life are mind and body altering, toxic substances, specifically drugs, alcohol and nicotine. Please don't dismiss this information as just another example of an adult trying to tell you what to do. Get the facts. Understand the implications and think about these issues. Drugs are widely available. You undoubtedly have been or will be pressured to "try" them. The choices are yours. The consequences can be devastating.

A. THESE SUBSTANCES KILL PEOPLE

Harmful drugs are chemical substances that change how your mind and body work. Drugs like heroin and cocaine are so harmful that they are illegal. But not all harmful drugs are illegal. Alcohol and tobacco, legally available to all adults, are also drugs. They alter the mind and the body, are addictive and, like illegal drugs, they can be deadly.

Data from The Center for Disease Control indicates that:

- 67,300 Americans died from drug overdoses in 2018. By 2021, that number had risen to over 100,000. An American died from a drug overdose every five minutes.

- Excessive use of alcohol causes approximately 88,000 deaths in the US per year.

- Cigarette smoking causes more than 480,000 deaths in the United States each year. Worldwide, tobacco use causes more than 7 million deaths per year. More than

87

10 times as many US citizens have died prematurely from cigarette smoking than have died in all the wars fought by the US. On average, smokers die 10 years earlier than nonsmokers.

According to the Alcohol Control Center, the nation's number one killer of persons between the ages of 15 and 24 is drunk driving auto crashes. A driver with a blood alcohol level of .10 is twelve times as likely to have an accident as one who is sober. The rate of suicides is 32 times higher for alcoholics than for non-alcoholics.

Using these substances is like playing Russian Roulette with a loaded gun. You <u>may</u> not die from one try, but if you persist, the results can be deadly. The temporary "high" is not worth the risk.

B. HEALTH EFFECTS

Even for the users who do not die directly from these substances, the impact on personal health can be horrendous.

According to the National Institute on Drug Abuse, in addition to the effects on the brain, illicit drugs can cause or worsen: heart disease, lung disease, stroke, liver malfunction, kidney damage and infectious diseases such as AIDS and hepatitis. Some drugs damage or destroy nerve cells in the brain and the central nervous system.

Alcohol can cause liver damage, brain damage, and is the fifth leading cause of cancer.

CDC data indicates that cigarette smoking harms nearly every organ of the body. Some of the effects include:

- Smokers are 25 times as likely to develop lung cancer as non-smokers.

- Smokers are 2 to 4 times as likely to suffer from heart disease.

- Smokers are 2 to 4 times as likely to have a stroke.

- Smoking can cause cancer almost anywhere in the body.

- The risk of developing diabetes is 30% - 40% higher for smokers than non-smokers.

C. BEHAVIOR MODIFICATION

All of these drugs alter brain functions and affect behavior. Often in ways that are harmful and foreign to the way you would act if you were "in your right mind".

Drugs and alcohol lead to loss of coordination, slowed reflexes, distorted vision, poor judgement, memory lapses and blackouts. They cause you to do stupid things. They destroy your ability to control how you act and what you do. You cannot consistently make good decisions while under the influence of mind-altering chemicals.

Some have the misconception that smoking marijuana is relatively harmless. Not so. In addition to leading to the step up to other drugs, marijuana use can significantly alter behavior. According to a study titled Marijuana Alert III: The Devastation of Personality, smoking marijuana creates "Pot Personality", the traits of which are: impaired short-term memory; emotional flatness, the dropout syndrome; diminished willpower, concentration, attention span, ability to deal with abstract or complex problems, tolerance for frustration; increased confusion in thinking, impaired judgement, and hostility toward authority. Do those sound-like characteristics that you want to "try on"?

The craving for harmful substances drives people to do things they would not do if not for the craving. There is a high correlation between drug abuse and crime. Bureau of Justice statistics indicate that 17% - 18% of federal & state penitentiary prisoners committed the offense that put them in prison to enable them to buy drugs, and that 50% have alcohol related problems.

The power to make choices is life's greatest gift. If you become addicted to something, you give up your freedom to choose.

When I was in college, I had a job as waiter and bartender for the president of the university, when he entertained guests in his home. One evening, after I served a soft drink to a male guest, a lady in his immediate circle asked him about his choice of beverage. I've never forgotten his reply. He said: "When I was in college, I played football. I decided not to drink then because I didn't want to impair my performance on the football field. After graduation I discovered that life is a much tougher game than football, and if I wanted to do my best, I better not start drinking."

D. DISTORTED SELF PERCEPTION

Drugs and alcohol distort the user's perception of personal capabilities and self-image. Users often think that their mental and physical abilities are enhanced when in fact they have been impaired. The most common example is not realizing the extent to which driving skills are impaired.

Many young males think that it is masculine and mature to drink or get high, that it makes them more mature, tough or more attractive to the opposite sex. Young ladies sometimes think it will make them more appealing to young men if they participate. In fact, it is neither macho or appealing to become loud, pushy and obnoxious, to lose control of bodily functions, or to puke up one's guts. All of which are frequent consequences of doing alcohol and other drugs.

E. ADDICTION

The term addiction comes from a Latin word for "enslaved". Being enslaved is not a good thing. Think seriously about whether you want to be enslaved to drugs, alcohol or nicotine. Use of these substances at an early age often leads to serious problems. One out of fifteen teen drinkers become an alcoholic.

According to a Harvard Medical School publication, addiction exerts a long and powerful influence on the brain that affects a person in three distinct ways:

- Craving for the object of addiction

- Loss of control over its use

- Continuing use of the addictive substance despite adverse consequences.

Addiction is a chronic disease that changes both the structure and function of the brain. Think about what your reaction would be if someone walked up to you with a scalpel and said "I want to alter your brain." That is what is happening when someone encourages you to "try" a potentially addictive substance. Studies by the National Institute on Drug Abuse confirm that these chemicals physically change the areas of the brain that are critical for judgment, decision-making, learning, memory and behavior control.

No one starts out by saying "I want to become an addict", but it is so easy to get caught up in the snare. These chemical substances affect the brain's pleasure, reward, learning and memory systems, making it easy to transition from the initial euphoria of the experience to becoming addicted to it; from liking it, to wanting it, to "needing" it.

Most addictions have their roots in the "gateway drugs"; alcohol and marijuana. These substances are harmful in themselves and often lead to more dangerous drugs. Studies of the brains of frequent marijuana users indicate that memory, the ability to solve problems, the speed of processing information and brain development are all impaired. Alcohol goes directly into the bloodstream and brain, altering thinking and body functions. Don't be trapped into rationalizing that I will only "do" the light stuff.

The pressure to "try" addictive substances can be strong. Reasons cited for starting are many:

- I want to belong – Peer pressure

- Everyone else is doing it

- I just want to have some fun.

- One time won't hurt.

- Life is boring - I want some excitement

- I'm curious to see what it's like.

- I have so many problems. I need an escape.

- I'm under so much pressure. I need a relief.

- To rebel against authority – "They can't tell me what to do".

None of these reasons are sufficient justification for giving up control of your mind and your life. There are better ways to deal with these issues.

Be particularly cautious of turning to drugs and alcohol as a means of escaping your troubles. When you are lonely and troubled you may be most vulnerable. Don't assume your miseries will go away because you temporarily escape into oblivion. Drugs and alcohol cannot make you more attractive, smarter, or more popular. Getting drunk or stoned will not solve your problems. The consequences only compound your problems.

Don't rationalize that: "It will never happen to me." "I'm strong. I can quit whenever I want. It's my life, I'm not hurting anyone else". Do not believe it! These chemicals are stronger than you are, and they change your willpower and your life. Many of the teens struggling through rehabilitation programs or suffering from the effects of these substances will tell you that they thought it couldn't happen to them.

The following are examples of typical comments by teens who lost control:

> "Once I started, I had to keep going. I could not control it. I had to have more."

> "I might never have recovered from my coma. I later thought 'why did I do that?' It wasn't worth it"

> "I was picked up for drunk driving. I fell down when the policeman asked me to walk a line. I spent the night in jail in my vomit drenched clothes. My mom cried when she picked me up."

"Once, when our source of pot tried up, we switched to beer. It didn't make me feel as good as pot, so I found a new and stronger drug. I was soon hooked. I had to have it"

"To buy the pot and beer I thought I had to have, I started stealing from the homes where I baby sat."

"Once I dried out and returned to somewhat sane behavior, I learned some things about alcohol and that I had a serious problem. For the first time since ninth grade, I felt a yearning to be normal."

Does this sound like a club you want to join? It's your choice.

Once started, quitting is not easy. For example: A National Institute of Drug Abuse survey of adult smokers found that 68% wanted to stop smoking. More than 55% had attempted to quit within the last year. Of those who attempted to quit, only 7.5% succeeded. The developed need for nicotine is strong, just as is the so easily developed need for other drugs.

Treatments for addictions are long, expensive and difficult. It is far better never to start.

F. EFFECTS ON OTHERS

Some rationalize that: "It's my life. What I do is nobody else's business". Nothing could be further from the truth. Drug abuse is not just about the abuser. Seeing a life destroyed causes anguish to parents, grandparents, siblings and friends. Younger siblings and friends copy what they see you doing, because they rationalize that if you're doing it, it must be ok. Your altered behavior can impact all those with whom you have contact.

A Point to Ponder: Have you witnessed a friend or acquaintance negatively impacted by drugs and alcohol?

Driving under the influence of alcohol or drugs can result in the death or crippling of passengers, or total strangers. Aside from the possible penalties involved, think about what having such an incident on your conscience for the rest of your life would mean.

On the worksheet in Appendix I, make a list of the names of the persons who would be affected if you were to become addicted to alcohol or other drugs. Think hard about whether you want to do that to them.

G. PEER PRESSURE

The pressure to go along with the crowd or a "friend", to do something you know you shouldn't do, can be severe. Peer pressure is the number one reason that people start using drugs. If you choose not to participate, you will likely be laughed at, dared and ridiculed. Labels like "loser" or "chicken" hurt but giving in means giving up who you want to be, to be what someone else wants you to be. "Giving in" means giving up control. The issue is "who is going to control your life?"

It may be useful to think of the worst case associated with both alternatives. The worst case of saying no may be name calling, shaming and ridicule by those applying the pressure and you feeling inferior and left out, not one of the crowd. The worst case of saying yes, can be addiction, with its myriad problems, and even death.

When someone tells you how "great" it is to get "high", they are telling only a part of the story. If they tell you it's fun and harmless, they are leaving out the part about consequences. Think about the consequences. They are not fun!

If a friend really cares about you, how you choose to deal with alcohol and other drugs will not affect the friendship. If your abstinence negatively affects the friendship, then the person cares more about you being like her/him than about you.

Recognize that those applying pressure are often doing so because of fear or guilt. They may realize that what they are doing is wrong and they may fear that you will reveal what they are doing. Or, they may secretly feel guilty and will feel better if you and everyone else is doing what they are doing. Don't let their problems become your problems.

Effectively dealing with the pressure takes forethought and planning. Be prepared ahead of time, so you don't do something you will regret. Always consider the consequences. A fundamental strategy is to avoid situations where pressure might be applied. If you know that a planned gathering is likely to involve drugs and alcohol, don't go. Other ways of coping without caving include:

- It is almost always better to <u>not</u> attempt to argue the merits of the action. That can be construed as judgmental by the person(s) applying the pressure, who clearly plan to participate. If you criticize imbibing, they are likely to take it as criticism of them personally. Just say "it's not for me".

- Have a list of excuses prepared. Blame your refusal on parents, coaches, you have to be somewhere, etc.

- Not tonight. I'm not feeling well.

- Suggest an alternative activity. If someone wants to drink or do drugs, propose some other idea for spending the time.

- Attempt to diffuse the pressure by asking lots of questions and then saying "I need to think about it".

- Simply leave the scene.

- Find a friend who shares your position and back each other up.

- Don't fall for the line that "everybody's doing it". Everybody is not doing it.

- Don't ride with someone who has been drinking alcohol or doing drugs. Find an alternative, even if it's walking. Don't put your life in danger for fear of offending someone.

Test your decisions about yielding to peer pressure against your values and goals. Ask yourself if doing what you are being urged to do conflicts with who you want to be. Remember that your life is more important than what your "friends" think of you. You have lots of things to do. True friends do not pressure friends to do things that are potentially harmful. If your friends do that, find some new friends. Drugs regularly destroy goals and dreams. Don't sacrifice yours for a temporary "rush".

The decision to "do" drugs can have devastating results. The choice is yours. Only you are responsible for you. When making a decision about harmful substances, remember to ask yourself if the choice fits with who you want to be. If you've started, you can stop. Find a counselor to help you stop. If you haven't started, think about the risks. Choose wisely.

The greatest travesty in America today is the lives ruined and/or lost due to drugs, alcohol and nicotine. The temporary "high" or satisfying the craving are not worth the consequences.

Please carefully consider taking the pledge outlined in Appendix J. Note that this is a pledge you make to yourself. No one needs to know which lines you checked or if you signed it. It is your choice. You <u>need not</u> show it to anyone. If you trust someone to keep you accountable, share it with that person. One element of character is keeping commitments you make to yourself. This is an important one.

PART VI.

CHOOSING A PROCESS FOR MAKING DECISIONS.

Using a rational process can help you make better decisions. Develop/identify an effective process and use it.

A. PROCESS CRITERIA

An effective decision-making process is one that satisfies the following criteria:

- It focuses on the real issues and needs.
- It encourages the gathering of relevant data.
- It is logical and widely applicable.
- It encourages the weighing of less-tangible considerations, such as values, goals and objectives, as well as facts.
- It encourages thoroughly thinking through alternatives, and possible consequences that will affect the decision maker and for others.
- It enables timely action.
- It makes enough sense to you that you will use it.

B. PROCESS OUTLINE

The proposed process incorporates twelve elements:

1. FRAME THE ISSUE
2. IDENTIFY THE INFORMATION NEEDED TO MAKE A GOOD DECISION
3. IDENTIFY VIABLE OPTIONS/ALTERNATIVES
4. CONSIDER THE LIKELY CONSEQUENSES/RESULTS
5. CONSIDER THE IMPACT ON OTHERS

6. TEST THE ALTERNATIVES AGAINST YOUR
    VALUES
7. TEST THE ALTERNATIVES AGAINST YOUR
    GOALS AND OBJECTIVES
8. TUNE IN TO YOUR INTUITION
9. THINK IT THROUGH
10. MAKE A DECISION
11. IMPLEMENT IT
12. EVALUATE PAST DECISIONS

While the proposed process is laid out in sequence, recognize that, to be most effective, it should be viewed as iterative. It is often beneficial to "loop back", to rethink previous conclusions as you employ the process. As you gather information you may see the need to redefine the issue. As you consider the consequences of your list of alternatives, you may realize that none of the consequences are acceptable, and thus you need a new list of options. At any point in the process, you may have an "aha moment", in which you see things more clearly. The solution may become obvious, or you may find it useful to backtrack and proceed from an earlier point in the process.

1. <u>FRAME THE ISSUE</u>

What's it all about? The first step in the decision-making process is to define or "frame" the issue. I use the word "issue" instead of "problem" on purpose. Much of what is written about decision making stresses "problem solving", and often equates decision making with problem solving. While problem solving requires effective decision-making skills, not all decisions involve problems. The word "problem" has a negative connotation not always useful to the process. Choosing between alternative job offers, both significantly better than your current job, is not a "problem". Choosing which of two good used cars to buy, is not a problem. We should view decisions, not as problems, but as <u>opportunities</u> of

100

two kinds: the opportunity to make the best of the issue at hand, and the opportunity to practice, (and thus improve), our decision-making skills. Defining the essence and scope of the issue is the foundation of a useful process.

Defining The Issue involves answering some basic questions:

- Why is a decision required?
- What is the real issue?
- What are the root causes of the issue/problem?
- How important is the decision?
- What are the real needs associated with the decision?
- What is your primary objective? What are your secondary objectives?
- What are the primary, real constraints?
- What are your wants/preferences associated with the decision?
- By when should the decision be made?

Why? Identifying why a decision is required helps define the issue and assists with answering other framing questions. "My teacher told me that he wants my project turned in by Monday, or I will get "O," credit, is a legitimate consideration when I decide how I am going to spend my weekend. It also established a deadline. Because I need reliable transportation to get to work, and my mechanic just told me my vehicle won't last long, drives the need for a decision about transportation. Understanding your motivation for making the decision will help you make better decisions.

What Is The Real Issue? Issues sometimes wear disguises. Following an effective process to the ideal solution for the wrong issue is not productive. Definition is critical. The way you define an issue can significantly influence your choices. A question of "should I buy the Sony or Samsung big screen

TV?", might more legitimately be defined as "should I make such a purchase at all?"

What is the Root Cause? If the issue is not a problem, why did the issue come up? If it is a problem, what is the root cause (or causes)? It is often useful to utilize the elementary technique of asking: "Why, Who, What, Where, When, and How".

How Important Is The Decision? A fundamental issue is deciding how much time and effort to invest in a decision, how rigorously to apply the chosen process. The more critical the consequences, the more you should invest in the effort. To facilitate the process, a system for assigning rankings can be useful:

1 Critical - These are the life-altering decisions that deserve your best efforts. (post high school education choices, career choices, spouse choices, choices about addictive substances, etc.).

2 Significant - These are the choices that have a major impact on the quality of your life but are not likely to completely change it. (buy a home in the suburbs or rent an apartment in the city).

3 Material – These make a difference, but don't have a major impact. (choosing a dude ranch or a beach resort for the next family vacation).

4 Mundane – These are the trivial choices we make every day. (what to have for lunch, which shoes to put on). They do not deserve a rigorous application of the process because the consequences don't matter much.

What Are The Real Needs? Distinguish between wants and needs. What results are really necessary to solve the problem or resolve the issue? Needs are basic. They represent what is required. The key is focus. For the best results, focus on the real needs. The more clearly you see the results you need, the easier it will be to identify and evaluate choices, and thus make an effective decision.

What Are Your Objectives? Objectives should address the real needs. Objectives define results to be accomplished in specific, measurable terms, with specified due dates. Aristotle said that "people are like archers. They need a clear target at which to aim". Clearly stated objectives help us identify what information we need, channel the development of alternatives and provide standards against which to test potential choices. It is not unusual to identify multiple objectives for major decisions. Prioritize objectives in terms of importance. Identify all your objectives, even those that conflict. You will need to address the conflicts in the analysis phase. Write down all that you hope to accomplish by making this decision.

What Are The Real Constraints? There are typically factors that limit the range of feasible choices. Money is a common constraint. A cap on the dollars available can limit the options. Time and geography can narrow the list of practical alternatives. Determine which constraints are "real". Question every identified constraint to determine if it is in fact restrictive or merely a "mental" barrier, a factor of limited vision. Brainstorm how constraints might be removed or rendered inconsequential.

A Point to Ponder: What other factors can be real constraints?

What Are Your Wants/Preferences? As humans, our emotions are real and relevant. That's ok. Making good decisions sometimes means resolving conflicts between wants and needs and thus requires tough choices. We should distinguish needs from wants, but it is unwise to treat decision making so mechanically that you ignore your emotions or the emotions of those affected by the decision. It is better to consciously acknowledge and consider your personal feelings and their impact on your choices than to have them unconsciously bias your thinking.

When? Time is often a critical factor, sometimes imposed by others or by circumstances. Identify precisely when a decision must be made. Hard decisions deserve ample time for analysis. Allow for sufficient time to utilize the process when dealing with important decisions. When circumstances permit, take control of the schedule and allow enough time to prepare for making the choice. Don't procrastinate until time pressures force you into making a poor or less than optimal choice. Putting off the analysis and the decision can mean that some attractive alternatives are no longer available or that someone else makes the decision for you. Give yourself a deadline.

Time and effort spent accurately defining/framing the decision issue will save time in the long run and provide a firm foundation for improving the quality of your decisions. Be thorough in defining the issue. Restate it in a number of different ways, until you are confident that you have it right. The best resolution to the wrong issue is not very helpful.

Writing down your issue definition is critical. It forces you to think it through. An "Issue Definition Worksheet" to help with defining the scope of the decision issue is shown in Appendix K.

> "The formulation of a problem is often more essential than its solution."
>
> Albert Einstein

2. <u>IDENTIFY AND GATHER RELEVANT INFORMATION</u>

Once you have the issue clearly defined, ask yourself: "what information would be useful for making this decision". Make a list of what you really need. For important decisions, it would be unusual for you to have in your memory bank everything necessary for making an effective decision. Additional information is usually required. Information is of three kinds: CRITICAL – information without which the decision should not be made (if at all possible), USEFUL – information it would be beneficial to have, if time permits, and IRRELEVANT – all information that has no impact on the decision. It is important to distinguish among the three types, to give priority to the critical and to refuse to spend time chasing the irrelevant.

> "The art of being wise is the art of knowing what to overlook."

> William James

Relevant information can be "hard", i.e. facts and figures, and "emotional" – how you feel about the issue and why you feel that way are relevant considerations. Both hard and emotional issues are important. Don't ignore either. It is especially useful to ask yourself why you feel the way you do about a subject. What is the source of your feelings? Consider how those affected by the decision are likely to feel about the issue. That nagging feeling may be your conscience telling you "something is not right here".

There are myriad sources of information: books, articles, the internet, experts (authorities respected in their fields) and personal observation/experience. Use them. Whenever possible and practical, verify what you read or hear before giving it credibility.

Be selective. Do not accumulate data for the sake of data or to put off having to make the decision. Develop, refine and use your list of what you really <u>need.</u>

"It is of the highest importance in the art of detection to be able to recognize, out of a number of facts, which are incidental and which vital"

Sherlock Holmes (Arthur Conan Doyle)

Know when to quit! Deadlines may dictate, but so should judgement. The time spent on gathering information should be related to the importance of the decision, and consideration of the "utility" of gathering additional information, i. e. at what point is the *value,* (improvement in the quality of the decision), of additional information insufficient to justify the *effort* to obtain more information? Keep asking yourself if more information will really enable you to make a more effective decision.

A Point to Ponder: What are some of the useful sources of information you would consider using to gather information about an issue?

3. IDENTIFY AND CLEARLY DEFINE ALTERNATIVES

After gathering relevant information, it's time to consider potential alternatives. The decision you make can be no better than the best alternative you conjure up, so time spent identifying options is usually well spent. This is an important step. Far too many decisions are unsatisfactory because the decision maker failed to consider enough options. Ask yourself "what are the alternative ways that I might meet my objectives?"

- Brainstorm. Be creative. There are almost always more options than initially come to mind. Think outside the proverbial "box".
- Don't evaluate options while creating. The key to brainstorming effectiveness is to suspend judgement when considering alternatives. Get as many options on

the table as possible. Postpone critiquing to prevent stifling creativity.

- Examine your assumptions about limitations. Some constraints are real, but some are only mental. Imagine that the apparent limitation did not exist. What could you do then?

- Begin early and plan time for breaks in the process. Your subconscious will keep wrestling with the issue and may well come up with a fresh concept.

- Review your experience. What worked (or didn't work) for you in similar situations? You should learn from all experiences, but don't slip into the rut of considering just the same old alternatives.

- Aim high. Don't just settle for incremental improvements. Set lofty targets.

- Imagine what a person you admire and respect would do in your situation.

- Think for yourself first, and then seek suggestions from one or more persons you admire and respect. Sometimes the process of explaining the issue you are facing to someone else will stimulate you to come up with a new possibility. A different perspective can be helpful, but never abdicate the development of your alternatives list.

- Keep reviewing your list. Any one idea may spark a thought about a related possibility.

- Consider combining alternatives to develop one even better.

Whatever the process you use for generating alternatives, list all the options that have a reasonable chance of working. Thinking through a comprehensive list helps you avoid impulsively pursuing the first idea that sounds good but may not be the best choice. Recognize that you cannot choose an alternative that you have not included in the analysis, and your choice can be no better than the best of those on your list. Identify as many reasonable options as possible.

Think beyond the obvious parameters. Your alternatives should be driven by your objectives but be sure your framing of the issue is appropriate. You may do a fantastic job of establishing and evaluating just the right alternatives for purchasing a new home in the ideal neighborhood, but if there is a reasonable probability that you will be transferred to another town in the next two years, renting should be included in your list of housing options.

Be very specific about the definition of the alternatives. Think them through and write them down.

4. <u>CONSIDER THE LIKELY CONSEQUENCES</u>

No one has perfect foresight. It is difficult to predict the outcomes of possible choices. However, to make better decisions, you must make a conscious effort to predict the consequences of your choices. Carefully estimating the probable results of each of your options will help you select the one that best meets your objectives.

The more clearly you understand the issue, your objectives and the consequences of your options, the higher the probability that your choice will be a good one. If you have accurately defined the consequences of your options, your decision will sometimes become obvious, without further analysis.

A Point to Ponder: What are some of the likely consequences of a decision to cut classes for a day?

Reflecting upon your careful definition of the issue and your specifically stated objectives:

1. Reject any that are clearly inferior. Refine your list of options to a manageable number, perhaps three to five.

Winnowing out those inconsistent with real constraints can help narrow the list. Ranking, prioritizing can help as well.

2. Attempt to imagine the most likely implications of choosing each of these short list alternatives. Write them down. Be very realistic, specific, and accurate. Don't kid yourself.

3. Consider the long-term impact of each of the options. Imagine how you would feel about the choice in a year, three years, ten years.

4. Use the hard data developed in your information search but reflect on it with logic and judgement.

5. Identify and acknowledge uncertainties. You won't know the consequences for sure until after the decision.

6. Ask yourself: what has to happen or not happen for this situation to turn out well? What are the consequences of being wrong?

7. Ask yourself if you can live with what might realistically be a worst-case scenario.

8. Consult with authorities you respect. A professional in the field (law, finance, medicine) may have a better grasp of the consequences of certain types of decisions than do you. For less technical issues, a trusted friend might serve as a sounding board.

9. Whenever possible, use scales that are objective, measurable, and meaningful and that reflect a reasonable level of precision for the subject being evaluated.

10. Narrow the list of options to those that come closest to meeting your objectives.

Keeping variables organized mentally is a challenge. It is almost always more effective to write things down. This is especially true when attempting comparisons. A worksheet like the one shown in *Appendix L* can be very helpful for visualizing and organizing information about possible consequences.

5. CONSIDER THE IMPACT ON OTHERS

People Matter! When considering the consequences of alternative decisions, pay particular attention to the consequences for others. Our decisions rarely affect only us. Think through who will be influenced by your decision and how they will be affected. Your choices can change lives, and not just your own. To help you understand the implications for others, write down the names of those likely to be impacted by your important decisions and the likely positive and negative effects on their lives.

A Point to Ponder: Can you think of examples of negative consequences for others that you didn't anticipate when making a decision in the past?

For many, a key life issue is finding the right balance between work and family life. If your family is important to you, your decisions should reflect that fact. Prioritize family in your time scheduling decisions. Demands on your time are infinite, but your time is finite. Make time for what is important to you.

Some decisions involve sacrifices. You may be perfectly willing to make personal sacrifices to take on and complete some task, because you value what you perceive to be the end result. Think carefully about the sacrifices others will have to make if you decide to pursue a particular course of action. Others who will be affected may not see the long-term benefits that you see or care as much about the outcome as you do. They may not be willing to make the sacrifices your decision will require of them.

Put yourself in the shoes of those who will be impacted by your choice. Treat them the way you would like to be treated.

110

When major decisions will impact others, get them involved in the process. Let them know what you are thinking. Share relevant information. Ask for, and listen to, input. Demonstrate a willingness to consider ideas and alternatives suggested by others. This does not mean that such decisions should always be made by consensus or majority vote. You should not abdicate decisions. Even if you have to make an unpopular decision, you will receive less resistance and more cooperation and commitment if those affected are informed and involved.

Using a worksheet like that shown in *Appendix M* can be helpful when thinking about the impact on others.

6. TEST POSSIBLE CHOICES AGAINST YOUR VALUES

Several years ago, Tony Campolo, a noted Christian author, who was the key speaker at a leadership conference I attended, related some research in which a group of mothers of Japanese children was asked: "if you could be granted one wish for your child, for what would you wish?" The overwhelming response from that group was that they would wish for their children to be "successful". When a group of American mothers was asked the same question, the overwhelming response was that they would wish for their children to be "happy". The question posed was a question about VALUES. Tony contended that both answers were inappropriate. What we should wish for our children is that they will be "GOOD". Being good means owning and practicing the right values.

Our personal values define the meaning of our lives. They define who we are and who we want to be. They often involve making choices about what is right and wrong and what is the responsible thing to do under the circumstances. To determine if a decision is "right" for you, you should test possible choices against your values. To test a decision against your values, you

111

must have previously considered and defined your ethical and moral standards and what core values are really important to you. That requires careful thought and is something that should be done with deliberation and great care, before you are faced with the pressure of making an important decision. By deciding now what is important to you, you will be better prepared to align your actions with your values in times of crisis or change.

In Part II, we talked about how to define develop and clarify personal values. Testing possible choices against your values should be viewed as a critical step in the decision-making process.

7. TEST POSSIBLE CHOICES AGAINST YOUR PERSONAL GOALS AND OBJECTIVES

Not all of your decisions will impact your personal goals and objectives. When one does, it is important to determine the likely implications each choice would have for their attainment. Of course, to test for implications, you must have defined your goals and objectives. If you haven't developed goals and objectives, DO IT NOW, before you have to make the next significant decision in your life.

No matter how expeditious a choice may appear in the short run, if it is inconsistent with where you want to go and what you want to be, it is not likely to be a wise choice.

When evaluating possible decision alternatives, ask yourself what impact that choice is likely to have on the attainment of your personal goals and objectives. Write down your goals and objectives, keep them available and consciously test alternatives against them. This practice becomes an effective means for weeding out unacceptable options and will help keep your life on track.

8. TUNE INTO YOUR INTUITION

Intuition sometime gets a bad rap because it is 'unscientific". It smacks of "having a hunch about which horse to bet on in the fifth race". It is very important not to confuse hunches with hopes. Do not let what you would <u>like</u> to have happen determine what you think <u>will</u> happen.

In fact, intuition accurately defined and applied, can be a great asset for effective decision making. If intuition is understood as drawing on a synthesis of one's <u>experience</u>, <u>knowledge</u> and <u>values</u> when making decisions, it can be a very useful resource. Intuition can be viewed as using what you know. We sometimes do not realize what all we know. Noted psychologists Carl Jung and Rollo May both wrote of intuition as the unconscious mind delivering data and experiences to the conscious mind. Think of your unconscious mind combing through every relevant experience you have ever had, every relevant fact you have ever learned and every personal value you have established and sending a summary by email to your conscious mind. Jung described intuition as "an unconscious ability to perceive possibilities, to see the global picture while addressing the local situation." So, intuition can also include concepts of creativity and perspective.

If intuition is to be useful, you must be careful about the facts, experiences and values stored in your unconscious. Intuition will only be as good as the data that feeds it. The reliability of intuition can be enhanced through reflection and meditation.

Give your subconscious/intuition time to work. Start early and schedule intervals in your conscious effort.

Ask yourself "What is my 'gut' telling me about this choice?"

A Point to Ponder: Has your conscience ever "warned" you not to go along with the crowd? What did you do?

9. THINK IT THROUGH

Checking your intuition does not mean that analysis should be ignored. Gathering and analyzing relevant information is crucial. The best approach is to utilize both reasoning and intuition.

Sound reasoning is the non-contradictory integration of evidence, experience, values, knowledge and objectives.

Accurately assessing a situation involves *being fully aware* of circumstances and alternatives, *applying* knowledge, understanding and educated instincts to your analysis, *weighing* the implications for others and carefully *evaluating* the possible consequences. Think it through.

"I think, therefore I am."

Rene Descartes

This is the point in the process to analyze and evaluate alternatives. Start by reviewing all the previous steps and asking yourself fundamental questions:

- Is the issue adequately defined? Have I identified the real need?
- Are my objectives clearly defined and will attaining the objectives satisfy the real need?
- Is my assessment of the importance of the decision accurate?
- Have I identified the constraints accurately?
- Have I accurately described my personal feelings and preferences? Can I objectively assess their impact on the decision?
- Do I have the information required to make an effective decision?

- Have I objectively eliminated unacceptable alternatives?
- Have I creatively and realistically identified the feasible alternatives?
- Have I adequately anticipated the consequences of each alternative?
- Have I adequately considered the impact of each alternative on other people?
- Have I adequately evaluated the consistency of each alternative with my values?
- Have I adequately evaluated the consistency of each alternative with my goals and objectives?
- If probabilities are involved in my analysis, have I included all possible options and realistically estimated probabilities?

Rigorously challenge each of the constraints. Are there ways to mitigate any of them? Reassess the alternatives. Has your work thus far stimulated the possibility of others? Would combining two or more result in a better alternative?

Be particularly sensitive to evidence that indicates an error in your thinking and be willing to correct such errors. Thinking can change thinking. That is one of the attributes that makes it so powerful.

Make any refinements indicated by this review.

Apply the criteria by which you will evaluate the alternatives. This is an important process because it forces you to think about what is really important to you and what is really relevant to the decision at hand. Make sure that the criteria accurately reflect your values, goals and concerns for the impact on others

Next, apply sound reasoning to evaluate the alternatives and the anticipated consequences. There are a variety of techniques for organizing and analyzing the alternatives to facilitate that evaluation. Several are described in Part VII.

Some Tips for Thinking Through Alternative Solutions

- Someone somewhere has dealt with this issue or solved this problem before (or one very similar). You don't always have to reinvent the wheel. Sometimes "best practices" are best practices for a reason, they work. Search for those solutions and determine if one or more can be adapted to your situation. (search the internet, reference books, query experts, etc.).
- Have you faced a similar situation before? Analyze what worked and/or what didn't?
- Break down the issue or problem into segments, deal with the segments individually and combine the solutions.
- If there is one particularly difficult element to the issue, separate it out. Apply the most rigorous analysis to that element. Having solved it, the rest become easier. If you can't solve it, don't waste time on the other elements.
- Combine two or more alternatives to build a "better" one.
- Consider "inverting" the elements of a possible solution. Change the sequence of steps to see if that improves the solution.
- Examine the possibility of using a potentially negative consequence of an option to create a positive effect that cancels out the negative.
- Identify ways to test the option before committing.
- If cost is a constraint, evaluate ways to reduce the costs through: substitution, removing non-essentials,

changing time schedules, changing sources, modifying specifications, etc.

- Check your conclusions against all available evidence.

Whether or not you use one or more "techniques" described, this step of the process, (as do all the steps) requires judgement. Good judgement comes from experience, education, logic and reason. Don't ignore judgment in favor of some formula. Apply good judgement to the process.

10. MAKE A DECISION

The time and effort you spend on various decisions will, and should, vary significantly. Two factors affect the appropriate time and effort involved; the expected consequences of the decision and the amount of time circumstances and pressures permit. Consciously match process time and effort to the impact the decision is likely to have. As soon as you have completed the analysis that the importance of the decision justifies, MAKE THE DECISION. Knowing *when* to make the decision is a critical element in making better decisions. You will almost never have all the information and time you would like. Reflect carefully on what you have and "pull the trigger".

Procrastination is the single greatest obstacle to effective decision making. Sometimes just getting started is the biggest hurtle. Start when you have enough time to complete the process. Allow time during the process to reflect, and to allow your sub-conscious to work. Avoid *Analysis Paralysis*. Don't get so bogged down in gathering and evaluating information that time and effort is wasted and/or time sensitive, viable and attractive alternatives are no longer available. Know when to start and when to quit.

Understand that not choosing is a choice. The opportunity may be missed or someone else may make the choice for you. Not deciding frequently leads to unsatisfactory outcomes. Take control. Make your own decisions.

A major reason for procrastination is FEAR.

- *Fear of Failure* – Some people have difficulties making decisions because of the fear of making the wrong decision. If you have followed an effective process and thought it through carefully, you have done the best you can do. Some of your decisions will fail. That in inevitable because you are human, but a majority of your choices will be good ones. Don't let fear of making the wrong choice keep you from making a choice. When you make a mistake, learn from it and move on.
- *Fear of the Unknown* – Some have difficulties dealing with uncertainty. The future is uncertain. Focus on what you do know, gather information and rely on experts to fill the gaps. Keep moving toward your goals.
- *Fear of Change* - Some are uncomfortable with change. They fear that change may mean they lose control. Everything in life changes. Everything! Change is another word for evolution. *How* we evolve is our choice. *That* we evolve is not. Life is a process of continuous change. If we don't change, we lose touch with reality. Learning changes (expands, alters) our minds. Change is how we grow. Your choices determine how you grow. Embrace change. Don't attempt to avoid it.
- *Fear of Rejection* – We hate to hear the word "no". We tend to take a "no" response to an idea, suggestion or choice very personally, interpreting it as a rejection of ourselves as well as the idea. Some go to great lengths to avoid hearing a "no", avoiding making decisions that might elicit a negative response. Listen carefully to a

118

"no" response. Ask why. There may be valid reasons that you hadn't considered and should take into account. Modifications may lead to a "yes". Don't let the possibility of a negative response deter you from making a decision.

In 1910, President Theodore Roosevelt included these remarks in a speech:

> "It is not the critic who counts; nor the man who points out how the strong man stumbles, or where the doer of deeds could have done them better. The credit belongs to the man who is actually in the arena, whose face is marred by dust, sweat and blood; who strives valiantly; who errs, who comes up short again and again, because there is no effort without error and shortcoming; but he who actually strives to do the deeds; who knows great enthusiasms, the great devotions, who spends himself in a worthy cause; who at the best, knows in the end the triumph of high achievement and who at the worst, if he fails while daring greatly, knows that his place shall never be with those cold and timid souls who know neither victory or defeat."

Mr. Roosevelt made a valid observation.

Focus on What is Important. There are typically only a few really important elements to a decision. Concentrate on the core issues. Ask yourself: what are the make or break elements of this decision? When having difficulty making a decision, ask yourself: "what's bothering me?" "What is it about this situation that is keeping me from promptly making the decision?" The answer will likely indicate where you should focus your attention.

11. IMPLEMENT

Once you have made the decision, develop a plan and implement it. Don't procrastinate. The best decision you can ever conceive is meaningless unless implemented. Identifying the best way to implement, will likely involve another set of decisions, decisions such as when and how. Apply what you have learned about decision making to the decisions about how to implement.

Develop an Action Plan. Write it down.

The value of a plan comes from engaging in the planning process. It forces you to think. It is unlikely that things will go exactly as planned, but with a plan, you are much better prepared to respond and adapt to the unexpected. The purpose of a plan is not to lock you into a rigid set of steps, but to prepare you to adapt to developments and effectively achieve your objectives. It also established a standard, a measuring stick, against which to measure progress and determine completion.

Ask yourself these questions:

- What has to be done to make this decision effective?
- Who has to be informed, of what?
- Who has to do what?
- From whom do I need assistance?
- What are the important interim and final completion dates?
- What resources/tools are required?
- How will I track progress?
- How will I measure results?
- What are my contingency Plans?

120

For some decisions, implementation is a simple one-step process. You decide and you do it. Others are more complex, involve multiple steps and require the involvement of others. To assist with those, an Implementation Planning Worksheet is provided in *Appendix N*. Be sure that the action plan includes periodic checks to see if things are on track, follow up steps that are required, coordination with outside persons or organizations and a final review to see that all bases have been covered.

Things do not always go as planned. It is useful to think about what you will do if problems arise, or things turn out differently than anticipated. Thinking through and developing plans for contingencies can help you adapt if the need arises.

A Point to Ponder: Think about what you will do if the outcome of a decision you made recently comes out differently than you planned.

Demonstrate a bias for action. Don't just sit there. Do something.

"I have been impressed with the urgency of doing. Knowing is not enough; we must apply. Being willing is not enough; we must do."

Leonardo da Vinci

"Perhaps the most valuable result of all education is the ability to make yourself do the thing you have to do when it ought to be done, whether you like it or not. It is the first lesson that ought to be learned and, however early a person's training begins, it is probably the last lesson a person learns thoroughly."

Thomas Henry Huxley

12. EVALUATE PAST DECISIONS

Don't succumb to the tendency to ignore or "forget" poor decisions and savor just the good ones. You learn to make decisions by making decisions. You will learn more about making decisions if you keep notes during the process and subsequently analyze both decisions that produced good results and those that did not turn out well. Ask yourself:

- What was the real reason I chose as I did?
- What are the real reasons this decision turned out well or poorly?
- Did I define the issue accurately?
- Did I consider all the realistic alternatives?
- What information should I have sought that I didn't?
- Was the information I used really relevant?
- Was there a way that I could have more realistically anticipated the consequences? What clues did I miss?
- What did I learn?
- Regardless of the results, what should I have done differently in the process?

Keep in mind that you must not judge choices solely by results. The quality of the process counts. "Good" decisions can have poor consequences and "poor" decisions may turn out well. The objective of the postmortem process is to learn some things that will help you make better decisions in the future.

Acknowledge your constructive decisions. Reflecting on the positives helps build confidence and self-esteem, which leads to better decision making. Ask: "what did I learn that I can apply in the future?" Analyze, don't rationalize, the dysfunctional ones. Ask: "what did I learn that I can apply in the future?"

Don't use the postmortem to beat yourself up for mistakes, but to improve your skills for making future decisions. You will never bat 100%, but, over time, making good choices will lead to better consequences and good decisions will lead to more good decisions.

Also bear in mind that it is not at all practical to review every decision. This analysis should be reserved for important decisions, those that have significant consequences.

> "Some of the best lessons we ever learn are learned from past mistakes. The error of the past is the wisdom and enabler of the future".
>
> Dale Turner
>
> "A man who has committed a mistake and doesn't correct it, is making another mistake."
> Confucius

Using the outline in *Appendix O* is a useful way of thinking about the evaluation of past decisions.

A Point to Ponder: Use the worksheet to review a major decision you made within the last year.

PART VII.

SOME USEFUL DECISION-MAKING TECHNIQUES.

In this section we will explore how to recognize, develop and apply some techniques and tools useful for decision making.

A. BRAINSTORMING

Brainstorming is a process that involves opening one's mind to the creation of multiple ideas, alternatives or solutions. Brainstorming as a thinking process can be a very useful tool to employ at various stages of the decision-making process. It is especially useful in the process of developing alternative solutions. Originally conceived of as a group process, where members stimulate each other to be creative by relating to and building on the ideas of others, the process is equally useful in individual decision making. The objective is to creatively identify as many ideas/alternatives as possible. The key to success is to avoid evaluation during the generation process. The initial objective is quantity not quality. The following guidelines have proved useful:

- Defer judgement during the generation phase. Criticism, even self-criticism, stifles creativity.
- Think creatively. Ignore typical constraints and limitations.
- Stretch your imagination.
- Shoot for quantity.
- Write down the ideas. Writing stimulates the creation of more ideas.
- Add on to refine and combine ideas to create new options.
- Allow time to pass between the generation phase and the evaluation phase.

124

The key is to avoid the limitations of traditional thinking and typical but limiting solutions. Be innovative.

> "Logic will get you from A to B. Imagination will take you everywhere."
>
> Albert Einstein

B. LATERAL THINKING

Lateral Thinking is a term coined by psychologist and consultant Edward de Bono to describe a series of techniques that he proposes for looking at the process of creating ideas and solving problems, by looking at them from a different perspective than straight forward logic. He contends that superior results can be obtained by training the mind to use these techniques, much as the mind can be trained to master concepts in mathematics. De Bono contends that there are almost always multiple ways to find a solution or solve a problem, but the approach requires unconventional thinking. His techniques have been incorporated into the training processes of many of the leading companies of the world, as well as many non-profit organizations. They can be employed by groups or by individuals.

> "Creativity involves breaking out of established patterns in order to look at things in a different way."
>
> Edward de Bono

De Bono describes multiple techniques for developing a deliberate, systematic way of thinking creatively in a repeatable manner. We will examine two of them here.

The Six Thinking Hats

Using this technique, the individual or group deliberately and systematically examines the issue from six distinct perspectives:

The White Hat

This perspective deals with gathering data and information.

- What information do we have?
- What information do we need?
- How and where are we going to get the information we should have?

Before considering solutions, we should have relevant information.

The Red Hat

This perspective has to do with feelings, hunches, intuition and emotions. These factors are always present. It is useful to acknowledge them and get them on the table.

- My gut feeling is that this will not work.
- I don't like this way of defining the issue.
- I feel strongly that there is only one right way to do this.

The Black Hat

This perspective deals with all the negatives and problems, the "what ifs". It is the cautionary perspective, employed for the purpose of preventing us from making mistakes, for identifying why something should not be done. The Black Hat can be very valuable but can be easily overused. Undue pessimism can kill promise.

- The regulations (laws) will not permit this.
- It would be unsafe.
- We do not have, nor can we practically obtain, the capacity to do this.

The Yellow Hat

The yellow perspective is for identifying all the benefits, the potential and logical positive outcomes. It looks for what makes these outcomes feasible.

- The potential results are "win-win".
- The benefits are long term.
- The return on investment is well above average.

The concern here is to be realistic while looking at the bright side.

The Green Hat

This is the perspective for creative effort, for overcoming obstacles and creating new approaches.

- Are there additional alternatives?
- Could we accomplish the same thing a different way?
- In what ways can the obstacles be overcome?
- What if we did this?

The Blue Hat

This perspective is for summary and overview, for checking that all angles have been adequately considered, for conclusions, decisions and action plans. This is the time to examine the thinking process to check for adequacy, to assure that all the perspectives have been thoroughly examined.

- So, here is the plan.
- _____ (who) will do _____ (what) by _____ (when).
- This is how we will measure results.

For both individuals and groups, the process enhances objectivity and thoroughness. For groups it reduces the potential for the discussion to deteriorate into argument, since all perspectives are jointly examined, and "feelings" are examined as part of the process.

There is no "right" sequence for the process. Sequence may vary by topic or preference. (If the hat language is too "cutesy" for you, consider alternative labels, such as the "yellow perspective".)

Alternatives

Creativity, in some ways, can be defined as a search for alternatives, for a better way, or the best way under current circumstances. A search for alternative solutions is often part of our approach to a new problem or new issue. However, we should not limit the search for alternatives to new issues.

Our tendency is not to look for alternatives unless there is a problem. We are usually quite comfortable with the old maxim, "if it ain't broke, don't fix it". Our traditional way of thinking insists that we show fault or a problem before we have a right to seek alternatives. This attitude often obscures significant opportunities for improvement. Even when current methods appear adequate, there may be a better way. Often, innovative new possibilities are the result of dissatisfaction with the status quo.

Our reluctance to seek a better way is often associated with the fact that seeking alternatives takes time and effort. Negative thinkers often complain that it takes more work to identify and consider more alternatives. That is true, but relevant only if you are sure that the best alternative is the first one considered. The rewards for considering more alternatives can be significant.

In some situations, there may be only a limited number of alternatives, but in most cases the number is only limited by the imagination we apply in designing them. Note that the concept of "design" is critical. We tend to limit our search for alternatives to finding existing solutions. We should identify "standard "ways of dealing with the issue first. But then, we need to expand our thinking to the process of designing new approaches, which can sometimes involve modifying or combining known alternatives.

Time is often a critical factor, so we cannot continue to look forever for the perfect alternative. The ideal idea is of little value if it is too late. A cut-off time for identifying alternatives must be established. At some point it is necessary to choose from the identified alternatives.

> "There is no doubt that creativity is the most important human resource of all. Without creativity, there would be no progress, and we would be forever repeating the same patterns."

> Edward de Bono

The following are some examples of situations that pose questions, the answers to which require the application of Lateral Thinking. Ponder them and see if you can come up with a solution.

The Tale of Two Pebbles

A poor farmer had the misfortune of owing a large sum of money to a local moneylender.

The moneylender was an ugly, vile person who fancied the farmer's beautiful daughter. So, he proposed a bargain. He would forgo the farmer's debt if the daughter agreed to marry him.

Both the farmer and his daughter were horrified by the proposal. So, the cunning moneylender suggested that they let fate decide the matter. He told them he would put a black pebble and a white pebble into an empty bag. Then the girl would pick one pebble from the bag.

1. If she picked the black pebble, she would become his wife and her father's debt would be forgiven.

2. If she picked the white pebble, she need not marry him, and her father's debt would still be forgiven.

3. If she refused to pick a pebble, her father would be thrown into jail.

When the moneylender bent to pick up two pebbles from the pebble strewn path on which they were standing, the sharp-eyed girl noticed that he picked up two black pebbles and put them in the bag. He then asked the girl to pick a pebble from the bag.

Careful analysis would indicate that there are three possibilities:

1. She can refuse to take a pebble – her father goes to jail.

2. She can refuse to take a pebble and expose the moneylender as a cheat – her father goes to jail.

3. She can pick a black pebble, sacrifice herself and save her father from debtor's prison.

What would you advise the girl to do?

The Man in the Bar

A man walks into a bar and asks the bartender for a glass of water. The bartender pulls a large revolver from under the bar, points it at the man's forehead and cocks the hammer back. The man says thank you and walks out of the bar.

Why did the man thank the bartender?

Trouble with Sons

A woman had two sons who were born on the same hour of the same day of the same month of the same year. But they were not twins.

How could this be so?

Lateral thinking resolutions to the above are as follows:

The Tale of Two Pebbles

The girl put her hand into the bag and withdrew a pebble. Without looking at it, she fumbled it and let it fall onto the pebble strewn path where it was lost among all the other pebbles.

"Oh how clumsy of me" she said. "But never mind, if you look into the bag for the one that is left, you will be able to tell which pebble I picked."

The Man in the Bar

The man had hiccups. He asked for water, a common cure for hiccups. The bartender recognized from his speech that he had hiccups. He used the gun to give the man a shock, another common cure for hiccups. It worked, so the man thanked the bartender and left.

Trouble with Sons

The two sons were part of a set of triplets.

The material above about Lateral Thinking was taken from Edward de Bono's book: SERIOUS CREATIVITY. Other techniques and information about Lateral Thinking can be found in that book, and De Bono's other books. He devoted one entire book to The Six Thinking Hats technique.

C. SCAMPER

SCAMPER is a creative thinking technique developed by Bob Eberle for use by school teachers. It can also be effective for developing additional ideas and concepts for resolving issues and solving problems. SCAMPER is an acronym of a process for identifying alternative solutions or resolutions:

Substitute: Replace some part of an identified option with something else

Combine: Join two or more elements of an alternative resolution to come up with what could be a better alternative.

Adapt: Try changing various parts of a solution to create new alternatives.

Modify: Change various attributes of an issue to determine if doing so suggests possible resolutions. (attributes may include: color, shape, size, position, texture, position, etc.).

Purpose: Consider other uses for the subject. Think about other ways it could function to achieve different results.

Eliminate: Arbitrarily remove one or more elements of the issue or a solution and consider the impact.

Reverse: Change direction or orientation.
Change/reverse the sequence of elements or steps.

D. PROS & CONS

One of the simplest techniques for evaluating alternatives is to list the alternatives with the associated pros and cons of each. You can then make a choice based upon your judgement of the best combination of pros and cons.

E. MATRIX ANALYSIS

Developing an Option Comparison Matrix can be very helpful for comparing alternatives.

This approach involves selecting the criteria you consider important to a decision and then comparing alternatives using those criteria.

The limitation of this technique is that it treats all criteria equally, when in fact that may not be so. The value of the approach is that it forces you to think about what criteria are really important to you and it organizes the data in a way that facilitates the comparison of alternatives

USING WEIGHTED SCORES IN MATRIX ANALYSIS. Not all criteria and objectives have the same value. Judgements based upon mentally attempting to juggle criteria can get confusing. Either explicitly or implicitly, we make judgements about relative importance. If the magnitude of the decision warrants it, taking the time to assign numerical values to the weights and multiplying the weights by the criteria score can help you make a more objective decision.

Assigning weights to the criteria can increase the probability of selecting the most effective alternative. The process for this approach is to:

1. Develop a list of decision criteria
2. Assign weights to the criteria on a scale of 1 to 10

3. Make judgements about how well each of the alternatives satisfies the criteria and assign a score from 1 to 100.
4. Arrange the data in a "Weighted Score Decision Matrix".
5. Multiply the raw scores by the weights
6. Add up the weighted scores
7. Consider the weighted total scores as a basis for making your choice.

The following is an illustration of how John might use this approach to evaluate job offers upon graduation:

WEIGHTED SCORE DECISION MATRIX									
		Job A		Job B		Job C		Job D	
CRITERIA	Weight	Raw Score	Wghted Score	Raw Score	Wghted Score	Raw Score	Wghted Score	Raw Score	Wghted Score
My "fit" with the people I've met	10	60	600	50	500	80	800	70	700
Quality/reputation of the company	9	50	450	40	360	80	720	30	270
Starting salary	6	50	300	80	480	60	360	70	420
Skills development/ Learning potential	8	80	640	70	560	85	680	40	320
Work schedule flexibility	4	70	280	55	220	90	360	35	140
Opportunity for advancement	7	65	455	90	630	75	525	55	385
Benefits	3	80	240	60	180	65	195	70	210
Total Wghted Score			2965		2930		3640		2445

Figure 2

This analysis indicates that the best place for John, given his preferences and perceptions, is Job C.

This technique can be adapted to situations where there are multiple persons involved in the decision process, e. g. where three siblings are making a decision about the best way to care for an aging mother, or a husband and wife are choosing

134

among multiple home purchase options. Each decision maker can complete a decision matrix and the results can be compared, debated and perhaps combined into one. (note that to work effectively, there should first be agreement about the criteria selected and the weights assigned to each criteria).

F. PROBABILITIES & EXPECTED VALUE

Probabilities. Many decisions deal with the future. The future is uncertain. Yet we constantly have to make decisions in the present, the results of which will depend on what <u>actually happens</u> in that uncertain future.

A helpful way of dealing with that conundrum is to think in terms of probabilities. Probability involves assigning a meaningful numerical value to the likelihood that an event will happen in the future. There are at least two dimensions to probability. Mathematical probability involves the prediction of outcomes from random actions or experiments. If you roll a single six-sided die, the probability of any one of the numbers one to six coming up on top is 1/6 or 16.6667%. If you roll the die 100,000 times, each *of the six numbers will come up pretty close to 16.67% of the time.*

Bayesian probability is a way of expressing, quantitatively, one's <u>degree of belief</u> that a certain thing will happen in the future. Most decisions do not involve six options with an equal probability of each occurring. You have to take the information you have, plus what you think you know and make a judgement about <u>how likely</u> it is that a particular thing will happen, or what the likely consequences of a choice might be. Getting your head around both these dimensions of probability will help you make better decisions. Assigning quantitative probabilities to future events and consequences will help you deal more effectively with the inevitable uncertainty.

You are perhaps most frequently exposed to the concept of probabilities when you listen to a weather forecast. When that TV prognosticator states that there is a 70% chance of rain tomorrow, what she is really saying is that "if conditions tomorrow are what we think they will be, there is a 70% probability that those conditions will produce precipitation". Note that both dimensions of probability are involved. Meteorologists do not know what tomorrow's conditions will be. Based upon past weather patterns, what the patterns are today to the west, north, south and sometimes east, and what they know about the way weather behaves, they predict what they believe the conditions will be tomorrow. They are applying Bayesian probability, expressing a belief grounded in experience and knowledge. Based upon their study of the way weather has behaved in the past, the atmospheric conditions they expect for tomorrow have produced rain 7,000 out of the 10,000 times those conditions have occurred. They are applying mathematical probability.

To think about probabilities effectively, you need to understand these basics:

- The range of probabilities is always: 0% (cannot happen) to 100% (absolute certainty).
- The sum of the probabilities of all possible outcomes must be 100%, never more, never less.
- When using probabilities to express a quantitative degree of belief, you must include all the possible outcomes in the analysis. You cannot realistically assess the probability of any one outcome unless you consider all possible outcomes. Probabilities must always total 100%.
- If there are multiple independent ways that an outcome might occur, the probability of the event occurring is

136

equal to the probability of the way with the highest probability:

- o If in November you are assessing the probability of supplementing your nest egg by enough to make a down payment on a new car in March, and you identify the possible sources of funds and their probabilities as follows:

  You make enough profit from a garage sale
  15.00%
  you receive a year-end bonus at work -
      40.00%
  your brother-in-law agrees to lend you the funds
  -     10.00%
  You hit the lottery -
            .001%

  Your probability of making that down payment is: 40%, because that is the probability of the event that could trigger the outcome which has the highest probability of all the events that could trigger the outcome.

- The math is different if multiple events <u>must all</u> happen to trigger an outcome.
  To determine the probability of two or more independent outcomes both/all happening, you multiply their individual probabilities together.

  - o Assume you are assessing the possibility of an investment in a particular stock doubling in the next year. You estimate that in order for that to happen, three things must occur, and the probability of each of those three things happening is as follows:

The total Stock Market must advance by at least 10%. Prob – 20%

The company must beat the Analysts' earnings per share estimates by at least 20%. Prob – 25%

The Federal Reserve must lower the discount rate by ¼ point. Prob – 20%

The probability of all three things occurring and your stock doubling in value is: (20% X 25% = 5%) X 20% = 1%

Note that the longer the "string" of independent occurrences that must materialize to produce a specific result, the lower will be the probability of that result.

Expected Value. Probabilities can help in dealing with decisions that have multiple, quantifiable consequences. The Expected Value of a choice is the weighted average of the possible values of that outcome, where the weights used are the probabilities associated with each consequence. The Expected Value is the sum of: all possible outcomes multiplied by the probability that the outcome will occur.

Assume that you have the opportunity to participate in a game of chance. This is a yes or no decision. It costs you $10 to participate. If you win, you get back your $10 plus varying amounts. After learning the rules, you calculate that the possible consequences and their associated probabilities are as follows:

1. You lose – probability 70%
2. You win $10 – probability 15%
3. You win $20 – probability 10%
4. You win $50 – probability 5%

Do you play or not play?

Expected Value Table			
Consequence		Probability	Expected Value
Lose $10		0.70	-7.00
Win $10		0.15	1.50
Win $20		0.10	2.00
Win $50		0.05	2.50
Total Expected Value			$-1.00

Figure 3

Note that this analysis does not tell you what decision to make. That might depend on how painful it would be for you to lose $10 at this time. It does not tell you what will happen if you play the game once. You might win $50. It does help you think rationally about the decision. What it does tell you is that if you played this game 1,000 times, you would probably lose about $1,000.

To learn more about probabilities and their applications for decision making, read: *PROBABILITIES IN EVERYDAY LIFE* by John D. McGervey.

You cannot "know" the future, but you can make informed judgements about what is likely to happen if you choose a particular course of action. Realistically understanding and considering probabilities and expected values will help you make better decisions.

PART VIII.

WHAT'S IT ALL ABOUT?

A. SPIRITUALITY AND RELIGION

At some point we all wonder what it all means. Why am I here? Does life have meaning? What is the purpose of life? What am I supposed to do? Does God exist? Why is there suffering and evil? Why is there something rather than nothing? What happens to me when I die? Beliefs about these kinds of issues define one's spirituality. As used here, spirituality is not the same as religion. Addressing issues of spirituality is an attempt to understand the essence and meaning of life. There is value in pondering these issues, for they help shape how we live our lives.

I firmly believe that one's spirituality/religion is very personal and a matter of individual choice. No one has the right to impose their beliefs upon another. That does not mean that it is wrong to share one's beliefs, but there is a huge difference between sharing and imposing.

Religions, unfortunately, have often been distorted and misused by humans for their own self-serving ends. Religion was the excuse for atrocities in the Crusades, the Spanish Inquisition, Catholic/Protestant conflicts in Ireland, persecution of the Jews, Jihad and other "holy wars". The official records of the Spanish Inquisition indicate that the Inquisitors burned alive 300,000 human beings because the victims held religious beliefs different from those of the Inquisitors. Political leaders of Germany, labeled a Christian nation, annihilated six million Jewish persons, because they were Jewish. Spanish priests enslaved Native Americans in the Southwest to build churches, allegedly to glorify God. The American Government and American religious denominations (churches) collaborated to wrench Native American children from their parents and homes to incarcerate them in boarding schools so they could be taught the missionaries' version of religion. The physical and psychological harm done those children was sometimes immense.

I believe that doing another person bodily or psychological harm in the name of "God" is an abomination. Any religion that preaches hatred or disrespect for others because of their beliefs is illegitimate. A valid religion should align us with moral truths, motivate us to do good works and develop character. It should help us live with problems that don't have easy solutions, and realities that don't have easy explanations. Its focus should be on principles that unite us, not doctrines that divide us.

Spirituality is a quest. Spirituality is a path. I believe that one's spiritual/religious beliefs and practices should be the result of one's personal quest, never dictated by others. I also believe that one should be open minded about things spiritual, willing to learn and to allow spiritual growth to occur as one learns. I am convinced that no one religious tradition has a monopoly on the truth. I am a seeker, convinced that spiritual understanding becomes deeper and more revealing through study, reflection, sharing in discussion and, most of all, through practicing what we believe. Think about the following questions concerning your personal spirituality:

1. How important should spirituality be in my life?
2. What are the important elements of spirituality?
3. What is the nature of God?
4. What is my relationship with God?
5. How can I learn more about the truth, knowledge and wisdom of things spiritual?

6. How important are creeds and beliefs to my spirituality?
7. What part do morals and ethics play in my spirituality?
8. Are a set of beliefs or how I live my life the most important aspects of my spirituality?
9. What part do personal values like compassion, gratitude and generosity play in spirituality?
10. What role does spirituality play in living a life of meaning?

A Point to Ponder: Consider writing down your current beliefs about your spirituality.

I share some of my thoughts about spirituality, not to convince the reader to agree with me, but to encourage her/him to think about what is really important.

I cannot believe, as do some, that persons are evolutionary accidents. I cannot believe it is an accident that the two cameras I have in my head, which I call eyes, can take two snapshots of the world I perceive and register it on my brain as a single image. I cannot believe that it is an accident that I can ingest flesh and plants that are turned into energy so I can work and play. I cannot believe that it is an accident that a sperm and egg can unite to form a new creature. I cannot believe that the powers and wonders of my mind are an accident. Some power, which I am at a loss to understand, enables those and other miracles to happen.

Science has revealed to us a lot about how the physical world works, about the vastness and wonders of space and the intricacies of the atom. That knowledge is a wonderful thing. It explains the "how" but not the "why". Science does not explain, nor is it intended to explain, why we are here or the meaning of life. The latter issues are for our minds to explore.

I accept that, at the core, there will always be a great mystery. We will never find all the answers. That is ok. I attempt to approach spirituality with a sense of awe. I find it helps to peer into the night sky and attempt to visualize the vastness of the universe, to savor the wonders of nature, and to gaze at a new baby and contemplate the miracle of birth, the creation of a new person.

Seek the truth. Understand that that you cannot hope to capture it all. Consciously make your spiritual decisions your own. Think about them, read about them, talk about them. Do not let someone else dictate what you believe. Be especially wary of those who claim to have all the answers. They don't. Beliefs are not irrelevant, because they influence our actions, but understand that true spirituality is not about what we believe, but about what we do, how we live.

Think about what role spirituality should play in how you live your life.

B. PURPOSE

Selecting a purpose gives our lives a reason for being and a focus. Our purpose should include a commitment to do something we consider meaningful and beneficial for humankind.

> "It's not enough to have lived. We should be determined to live for something."
>
> Dr. Leo Buscaglia

It starts with identifying the right path to walk, the right way to live, and then selecting a purpose to which one is willing to devote one's efforts. Ask: what does the world need that I would feel good about providing? If one has a worthy purpose, a plan and the persistence to pursue that purpose, it makes life worth living.

143

"They say there are two important days is your life: the day you were born and the day you find out why you were born.

Carl Townsend.

Having a purpose does not guarantee that life will be easy. Learning to cope with adversity and suffering builds strength. What is important is, not the circumstances that befall us, but how we respond to those circumstances. The key question is not "is the path easy", but, "is the path worthwhile". We should periodically stop and access our significant experiences, good and bad, and ask:

- "What did I learn from that?"
- "How can I use what I've learned to keep making progress?".

"We're here to add something, to construct, to preserve. To leave something good for those little ones who are going to come into our world. Let that motivation be so firmly established in your heart and mind that you can say, 'I will stand for this. I will live for this."

Bear Heart – Muskogee Creek, Native American.

In Viktor Frankl's book, *Man's Search for Meaning*, about the plight of Jews in the Nazi death camps of WW II, Frankl relates that he survived, but lost his wife and parents to the atrocities. From that experience, Frankl, a psychotherapist, developed a thesis that contends that others can control everything about a person but that person's attitude.

Frankel credited his survival, and that of others, to adhering to the principles of: choosing an undefeated attitude, committing to values and goals, fulfilling one's responsibilities, serving others, demonstrating courage, seeking peace and pursuing happiness in the face of adversity. Later he stressed these principles in his psychotherapy practice and espoused them in his writings.

> "Don't go after happiness; rather commit yourself to something bigger than yourself, and let happiness come chasing after you."

> Viktor Frankl

C. MEANING

How we perceive the purpose of our lives and what gives our lives meaning affects our decisions. Much has been written about the attempt to answer the question: "What is the meaning of life?" That question is too abstract. More useful questions are: "What gives life meaning?", and "What can I do to make my life meaningful?" These are important questions, for how we answer them determines how we focus our lives, how we spend our time and energy and ultimately the value, the worth of our lives. The word "meaning" has two overlapping dimensions. The first has to do with purpose. Something has meaning if there is a purpose behind it. The second dimension has to do with significance. Something is meaningful if it makes a difference. Our lives have meaning if we live with the purpose of making a positive difference in the world, and particularly in the lives of others.

> "To be what we are and to become what we are capable of becoming is the only end of life."

> Robert Louis Stevenson.

We are programmed to want our lives to have meaning. Our lives will be meaningful if we accept the responsibility for making them so, and if we work at it. "Working at it" can be outlined as a process:

- Develop a vision of the person you would like to be, the kind of person you would be proud to be. Write down that vision.
- Think through what you would need to do to make that vision a reality. Write down those things.
- Make decisions. Take action.
- Reflect on your experiences. To what extent did you guess right? What did you learn? Did your decision help you become, or detract from your becoming, the person you want to be?
- Weigh and apply what you learned as you make your next decision.
- Repeat the previous three steps.

Meeting your standards should be challenging. You will never achieve the ideal, but your life will be more meaningful, interesting and fun for having employed the process.

> "The meaning of life is not to be found in having lots of money, fame, prestige or stuff. It is to be found in living a worthy quest for positive achievement. Make a difference in the lives of other people, make a difference for good. Create new relationships, new feelings, new forms of goodness in the world, by what you do and who you are. You will find in that process a sense of fulfillment that we so often seek in all the wrong places."

> Tom Morris

> "Beyond work and love, I would add two other ingredients that give meaning to life. First, to fulfill whatever talents we are born with. Second, we should

146

try to leave the world a better place than when we entered it."

The Search for Meaning - Many of us live lives, not of <u>quiet</u> desperation, (as Thoreau described), but of a <u>clanging</u> desperation. We are stressed daily by stories of man's inhumanity to man and evidence of a global environmental crisis that raises legitimate questions about the ability of our planet to long sustain life as we know it. Many have become disillusioned by our modern culture's pervasive emphasis on materialism. Owning more things never seems to be "enough". Pressing schedules make it seem like "there is never enough time".

It is important to understand that everything one says and does has consequences.

> "No teaching for the path of action could be more fundamental or primary than the teachings of love and respect – for oneself, for one's world and for the Great Spirit, which is all life in all things. The aspirant can perform no greater service for his world than to be mindful that his acts, even his thoughts and speech, become a part of the condition of the world."

Rolling Thunder – Cherokee

Many are searching. Some search for answers in all the wrong places. Some would like answers but won't make the effort to search. To some, despite feelings of emptiness and desperation, the idea of searching never occurs.

Consciously or unconsciously, we wonder about the meaning of it all.

147

"Life has been given to us not so that we can spend it in idle enjoyment. No, life is a struggle and a series of battles: the struggle of good with evil, of fairness with injustice, of freedom with oppression, of true love with desires of the flesh. But we need to remember this not merely in order to criticize contemporary life, but so as to establish a better life for all. We need to believe that life has to be better than it is at present, and to live our lives in such a way as to make it better."

Leo Tolstoy

The search for meaning should be based on understanding that everything is interdependent. Humans must be aware that everything they do impacts other beings, and that, at least part of one's purpose is to help take care of others.

Meaning is to be found by living the "right" way. One has many "roads" from which to choose. Choose to travel the "right road". This means living one's life consistent with the principles and values of:

- reverence for the Sacred
- truth
- integrity
- honor
- balance & harmony
- compassion
- generosity
- courage
- respect for the rights and ideas of others
- reverence for nature
- respect for elders
- personal responsibility
- patience
- perseverance.

Finding meaning involves selecting a set of values and principles, living a life consistent with those values and principles, selecting a worthy purpose and pursing that purpose to the best of one's ability. Living meaningfully, also requires that we accept responsibility for our actions, recognizing that we are co-creators of our lives through the choices we make. To find meaning, to live well, we must determine why we live, a purpose, and then really <u>live</u>.

One of my high school friends emailed this to me. I don't know the name of the author. It expresses some significant truths. I thought it worth sharing.

<u>THE TRAIN OF LIFE</u>

"At birth we boarded the train and met our parents.
We believed they would always travel by our side

However, at some station our parents will step down
from the train,
leaving us to journey alone.

As time goes by, others board the train and they
become significant,
e.g. our siblings, friends, and even the love of our life
and our children.

Over time, many will step down and leave a permanent
vacuum.
Others will go so unnoticed that we won't realize they
have vacated their seats.

The train ride will be full of joy, sorrow, fantasy,
expectation, hellos and goodbyes.

*A successful journey comes from having a good
relationship with all passengers,
requiring that we give the best of ourselves.*

*The mystery, for everyone on the train, is not knowing
at what station we ourselves will step down. So we must
live in the best way we know how; loving, sharing,
forgiving and offering the best of who we are.*

*It is important that we do this, because when it is our
turn to step down and leave our seat empty, we should
leave behind beautiful memories for those who continue
the journey. The train will go on.*

*I wish you a joyful journey on the train of life. Reap lots
of success and give lots of love.*

I thank you for being one of the passengers on my train.

*People will forget what you did. People will forget what
you said.
But people will never forget how you made them feel. "*

D. WISDOM

Wisdom is not about developing a specific proficiency or skill.
It is about learning how to live. Achieving wisdom involves
developing the ability to understand the real meaning of the
ordinary and extraordinary things that happen in one's life. The
acquisition and demonstration of wisdom is worthy of being
one of life's highest aspirations. Seeking wisdom is a quest.
The prime motivation for seeking wisdom is to develop the
ability to determine the "right" way to live one's life, to
consistently make effective decisions.

Wisdom involves the accumulation of knowledge and, more
importantly, the understanding of how to apply that knowledge.
Learning is an essential and lifelong pursuit. Accept

challenges. Explore the unfamiliar. Practice healthy skepticism. Ask questions. Questions lead to truth. Our goal should be to learn enough truth to have wisdom, to apply the right principles at the right time.

Many subscribe to the wisdom of the Buddha. The Buddha taught that wisdom is based upon:

- The Right View – seeing life as it really is, not as it appears or as you would like it to be.
- The Right Intentions – dealing with others with understanding and compassion.
- The Right Action – do no harm.

His teachings include Four Noble Truths, the application of which provide a prescription for healing, and for problem solving:

- Diagnose the problem.
- Identify the underlying causes.
- Determine the prognosis.
- Prescribe a course of treatment.

He taught that the causes of many problems can be traced to "The Three Poisons":

- Ignorance
- Desire
- Aversion

Hope is expressed in his contention that:

> "Every sentient being has the potential to improve and become enlightened."

Develop Wisdom - There are multiple, complex and interrelated elements to the development of wisdom:

- Spirituality is at the core of wisdom.
- Self-knowledge is fundamental. To see the world clearly, one must first understand oneself.
- Understanding, and applying, the right principles and values to all decisions are basics.
- Wisdom is acquired through experience, but experience does not automatically generate wisdom. It is the ability to reflect upon and learn from experiences that confers wisdom.
- Awareness and mindfulness are important to effective understanding and reflection.
- Receptivity to new ways of thinking and ordering facts and knowledge enhances wisdom.
- The ability to find balance and harmony between apparently conflicting objectives and perspectives helps develop wisdom.
- Compassion, focusing on the "common good" rather than self-interest, indicates wisdom.

Experiences contribute to wisdom. Life grants us wisdom, often in ways we do not initially understand or choose. Observation, awareness and listening are essential skills for developing knowledge. Integrity, personal character and good judgement are essential for applying that knowledge effectively. The fruits of wisdom are the calmness and peace of mind which come from self-control. Abraham Lincoln remarked that "I do not think much of a man who is not wiser today than he was yesterday." Wisdom comes from making the most of the opportunities for learning which life offers every day.

Wisdom must be tempered with compassion. To see things clearly requires viewing life through the "eye of the heart". The application of real wisdom requires the balancing of head and heart.

E. LOVE

The essence of a life of meaning is Love. Identifying what we love, paying attention to what we love, doing what we love, sharing what we love, these are the factors that make life worth living. What we choose to love motivates us, moves us forward, shapes our lives, satisfies our longings. Love keeps us awake and alive.

> "and now these three remain: faith hope and love. But the greatest of these is love."
>
> 1 Corinthians 13:13

When we know what we love, we achieve a clarity of purpose and the capacity to act on what we believe. What we love we pay attention to.

> "Attention is the tangible measure of love. Whatever receives our time and attention becomes the center of gravity, the focus of our life. This is what we do with what we love: we allow it to become our center."
>
> Wayne Muller

What we choose to love is, of course, critical. We should love family, friends, ourselves, truth, integrity, beauty, serving and life. We should love what brings us and others benefit, not what brings us harm.

How we love is equally important. Real love is unconditional. If our love is dependent upon another behaving a certain way or doing a certain thing, it is about loving ourselves, not the other person. Love is being real and caring, being there for someone.

No matter our state of well-being, no matter how dire our circumstances, we all have the capacity to love. Exercising that capacity enriches our lives as well as the lives of those who are the recipients.

Ideally, we should love everyone, even those hard to love, or even like. That is extremely difficult. If we can't bring ourselves to love the rascals of the world, we should at least treat them with respect and compassion. We should also abandon any expectation that our acts of love will be reciprocated. It's not likely to happen. We should not make our acts of love conditional.

Mother Teresa, the nun and missionary who dedicated her life to alleviating the suffering of the "poorest of the poor", who was awarded the Nobel Peace Prize and canonized as a Saint, had these things to say about living a life of love and meaning:

> *"People are often unreasonable, illogical and self-centered: Forgive them anyway.*
>
> *If you are kind, people may accuse you of selfish, ulterior motives.*
> *Be kind anyway.*
>
> *If you are successful, you will win some false friends and some true enemies.*
> *Succeed anyway.*
>
> *If you are honest and frank, people may cheat you.*
> *Be honest and frank anyway.*
>
> *What you spend time building, someone may destroy overnight.*
> *Build anyway.*
>
> *If you find serenity and happiness, there may be jealousy.*
> *Be happy anyway.*

The good you do today, people will often forget tomorrow.

Do good anyway.

Give the world the best you have, and it may never be enough.

Give your best anyway.

You see, in the final analysis, it is between you and God. It was never between you and them anyway."

Great advice from a wise lady who had the integrity to practice what she preached. Go thou and do likewise.

PART IX

YOU CAN MAKE BETTER DECISIONS

It is useful to follow a rational process and employ practical tools, but even more important is what we bring to the decision-making process.

We all approach decision making from the perspective of our individual levels of knowledge and experience and our own unique set of assumptions, paradigms, values, aspirations, attitudes and prejudices. These factors reflect our understanding of how the world works and how people behave. They form the context within which we make decisions and have a profound, and often unrecognized, impact on the quality of our choices.

It is imperative that our understanding, of the way things work and why people do what they do, matches reality and truth as closely as possible. This does not happen automatically. It takes effort, reflection and wisdom.

You can make better decisions if you practice the following guidelines.

A. SHARPEN YOUR DECISION-MAKING SKILLS.

1. Recognize the Importance of Decision Making.

Decision making is the most important thing you do. When considering important choices, ask yourself: "does this choice reflect <u>who</u> I want to be". You create yourself through the decisions you make. Every choice you make is a decision, not only about what to do, but a decision about **Who You Are**.

Making better decisions requires both intention and attention. Effective decision making starts with awareness. Be aware that a decision is required and give the decision the attention it deserves. Decision making is a critical life skill, a skill that can never be perfected, but can be developed and significantly enhanced. You can make better decisions, if you want to do so enough to work at it. The meaning of your life, your achievements, your happiness and your self-satisfaction all depend largely upon the choices you make. Recognize that this is so, and treat decision making accordingly.

It's your life. You are the one who should, whenever possible, make the decisions that affect it. Don't abdicate choices that should be yours, and always take responsibility for the decisions you make. Be sensitive to the significance of your decisions and develop the self-discipline to invest in each decision the effort it warrants. You take constructive ownership of your life through the choices you make.

2. Seek Knowledge, Truth and Wisdom

Knowledge is important and useful. Knowledge involves the awareness and understanding of facts, information and skills (knowing how to accomplish certain tasks). Knowledge is typically acquired through education and experience. Plato defined knowledge as "justified true belief". We should gain all the knowledge we can.

> *"Knowledge does not mean mastering a great quantity of different information but understanding the nature of the mind. This knowledge can penetrate each one of our thoughts and illuminate each one of our perceptions."*
> Matthieu Ricard

We most often use the word "truth" to describe something that conforms to reality, something that is authentic or factual. It is also used to refer to the opposite of falsehood, as in telling the truth instead of lies. The search for truth is an attempt to determine the way "things really are". The truth can never be totally possessed, only pursued. But that in no way diminishes the value of the search. The pursuit is a worthy and rewarding one. Truth matters.

> "Wisdom is not a product of schooling, but of the lifelong effort to attain it."
>
> Albert Einstein

Knowledge is valuable but, by itself, insufficient for effective decision making. Making better decisions requires wisdom. Wisdom is more than intelligence, knowledge or understanding. It means using these tools to think and act in ways which demonstrate sound judgement, and which produce choices that are beneficial and productive.

> "Knowledge is of no value unless you put it into practice"
>
> Anton Chekhov

You don't get wisdom out of a textbook. We can't get enough knowledge to make us wise. Wisdom is the effective use of knowledge. Wisdom involves the application of intelligence, knowledge, compassion, self-discipline and value principles to the decision-making process. We attain wisdom by developing the expertise to deal with the difficult questions of, and by adapting to the complex requirements of life. It involves determining the "right" thing to do and having the courage to do it. Our goal should be to become wise decision makers.

Acquire knowledge. Search for the truth. Develop and practice wisdom.

> "A good head and a good heart are always a formidable combination."
>
> Nelson Mandela

3. Develop and Apply a Process

Using a systematic, practical process will help you make better choices. Such a process is outlined in this book, as are a variety of tools and systems for improving the quality of decisions. It is not practical to follow the entire process for every decision. Minor decisions do not justify rigorous analysis. The process is designed for decisions with significant ramifications. Even for important decisions, the answer may become obvious at some point during the process. Try the process. Try the tools. Refine them. Find out what works best for you. You should not attempt to apply the entire process and every tool to every decision. Quickly think through the process with your issue in mind, to gain an overall perspective. Then focus on what matters most. Frame the issue and determine which process elements are most relevant to the current decision, and which therefore should receive the bulk of your attention.

The purpose of this approach is not to make decision making mechanical, but to help you:

- understand the critical importance of decision making
- understand that decision making is a skill that can be improved,
- think seriously and creatively about the process
- resolve that you will become a better decision maker.

4. Evaluate the Importance of Your Decisions.

Before tackling an issue, carefully assess the short- and long-range impact of possible consequences, to determine how much time and effort to invest in the process. Consider using the "Critical, Significant, Material, Mundane" ranking system described in PART VI. Trivial decisions don't warrant detailed analysis. Match effort to importance, after thinking through the long-term implications. What may initially appear trivial may have significant long-term effects, e.g. a decision to ignore "minor" ill-health symptoms can lead to major problems.

5. Carefully Consider the Context.

Decisions are not made in a vacuum. Your choices are affected by circumstances, your worldview, your values, your goals, your objectives and how you define your priorities. Looking at events in their full context is a critical requirement of rational decision making. Examine carefully the realities of the situation. Refine those components of the mental context within which you make decisions, to make sure they are what you want them to be. The effort will help you make better decisions.

6. Develop Your "Systems Thinking" Abilities.

Systems Thinking is the discipline for seeing the whole picture. It provides a framework for identifying cause and effect and other relationships, for seeing patterns, for recognizing interdependencies. Look for root causes. Look for the systems that created the current situation. Treat causes rather than symptoms.

> "You never change things by fighting the existing reality. To change something, build a new model that makes the old model obsolete."
>
> Buckminster Fuller

7. View the Situation from the Other Person's Perspective.

It can be difficult to be objective and rational about a situation in which you are emotionally involved. Empathize, put yourself in the other's shoes. Reach out – "you seem to see things differently. I need to understand. Tell me more."

It can also be useful to mentally remove yourself from the decision and treat the situation as if a friend had described the circumstances and asked you for advice. This process may help you more readily see the situation from multiple perspectives and to be creative in thinking about alternatives and win-win solutions.

B. FOLLOW YOUR CONSCIENCE.

Mold a strong character and make decisions that are consistent with your character.

1. Act Morally and Ethically.

Carefully establish your moral and ethical standards and stick to them.

2. Seek and Tell the Truth, Always.

We can never know the whole truth. Nevertheless, we should seek truth. The value is in the search, the striving, and in the satisfaction of knowing you have found a piece of it.

Believing does not make things true, nor does denying that something is true make it false. Some things, like gravity, are just naturally true, whether we believe them or not. Denying that gravity exists does not cause us to fly off the earth. Some things are not true, and never will be, no matter how earnestly we want them to be true.

We face a particular challenge today. We are bombarded daily by information, and conclusions based upon that information, from our smartphones, computers, televisions, newspapers and magazines (at least for those of us who still read newspapers and magazines). We hear and read a lot about "fake news", (during World War II, it was labeled propaganda). A lot of the information is contradictory. How can we possibly decide what is "true"? How should we test what we hear and read?

There are no concrete answers to those questions. One can only apply informed, rational judgement. Asking the following questions and thinking about the answers is often useful:

- Are the information and conclusions consistent with what I think I know about the subject?
- Is it logical? Do the conclusions reasonably follow from the premises?
- Is the information consistent with my experience?
- Is the source reliable? Have the information and conclusions offered by this source in the past been accurate?
- How can I cross check the information with other sources? How does it compare?
- What are the logical consequences of believing the information and "buying" the conclusions?
- Are believing and buying consistent with my values and principles?

3. Care About People.

People matter. Be ever aware of the impact of your decisions on others. Almost all your decisions affect other people. Treat people with dignity and respect. Things are to be used, people are to be loved. Loving things and using people inevitably lead to poor decisions.

Don't confuse morality with legalism. Doing what is "right" does not always mean doing what conforms to the rules. The legalist who proclaims that one should "do what is right even if the sky falls down" would be on the right track if he didn't confuse "right" with conforming to rules. Rules/laws are important. The alternative is chaos. We have a moral responsibility to follow rules, to preserve order. But, rules, even intelligent rules, cannot anticipate every possible situation. We have a moral responsibility to do what is "good" for people. Sometimes, following value based principles may be more "right" than following the rules. The two principles that will serve you well in making choices that impact other people are: *Agape* (love) and *Sophia* (wisdom). Well-reasoned compassion is almost always the best choice. Ask yourself two basic questions: "Does this choice reflect Who I Want to Be as a Person?" "What is the Compassionate thing to do in this situation?"

4. Practice Personal Integrity.

Ensure that there is congruence between what you know, what you profess, what you say, and what you do. Tell the truth. Honor your commitments. Demonstrate in actions the values you profess to admire. It is by practicing integrity that you earn trust and trust is critical to human relationships.

5. Accept Responsibility.

You are responsible for who you are, what you do, what you say, how you treat people and how you live your life. You are responsible for the consequences of your decisions. Accept your personal responsibilities.

6. Meet Commitments.

Resolve to always do what you say you will do or have an obligation to do. Demonstrate that you can be relied upon. Doing so earns you the respect of others and yourself.

7. Respect and Preserve Our Natural World.

Environmental quality and the quality of human life are mutually dependent. Preserving nature from the destruction of human endeavors is our moral obligation to this and future generations. We have no right to destroy the planet our grandchildren and their grandchildren will inherit. We are meant to be stewards, not exploiters, of the beauty of creation and its life giving and life enhancing functions.

The challenges of responsibly utilizing Nature's abundance are daunting, but what is inexcusable is the rampant and wanton abuse of nature for no reason at all, other than human indifference, laziness and sloth. This indifference, the mindset that "it doesn't matter", is the greatest threat to the richness and beauty of our earth.

Choices, about the goods we purchase, about production methods, about lifestyle and life practices should be consistent with the principles of "Sustainability". Sustainable products and practices are those that are environmentally friendly from extraction and creation through disposal or termination. Choose those options that render no permanent damage to the environment. Make sustainability and preservation a conscious part of your decision making.

"Man must be made conscious of his origin as a child of Nature. Brought into a right relationship with the wilderness, he would see that he was not a separate

164

entity endowed with a divine right to subdue his fellow creatures and destroy our common heritage, but rather an integral part of a harmonious whole. He would see that his appropriation of earth's resources beyond his personal needs can only bring imbalance and beget ultimate loss and poverty for all."

Linnie Marsh Wolfe

C. SHARPEN YOUR PERSONAL SKILLS.

1. Learn to Learn.

Be a learner. No matter how it turns out, every experience has something to teach you. Reflect on your major decisions and the consequences. In anticipation of an experience, contemplate: "what should I learn from this?" After each experience, ask yourself "what did I learn from that?"

"Live your life as though you were to die tomorrow. Learn as if you were to live forever."

Mahatma Gandhi.

Develop a learning mindset. Learn to learn. It is a skill that can be developed and improved. Develop an interest in acquiring knowledge. Ask lots of questions; to yourself and to others. Learning is more than schooling. It is a state of mind, a willingness to consciously look at the world and life with an alert sense of curiosity and wonder.

With a learning mindset, setbacks are not failures. They become data that can be framed into opportunities to learn, to improve. The first time a child touches a hot stove, the child learns something. That information is stored in a data bank that is useful for shaping future decisions. Every experience has that potential, but the process is much more effective if you make a conscious effort to learn from your experiences.

Curiosity - Consciously strive to develop a healthy curiosity. It is a trait that can be developed, and can broaden knowledge and perspectives. Try new experiences. Explore new places. Ask "why" questions. Curiosity generates energy, gets us involved in life, facilitates learning, uncovers opportunities and adds to the quality of our lives. A prime driver of learning is the search for answers to life's questions. The questions that engage our minds reflect our interests and influence the direction and quality of our lives. Curiosity can be developed if one has the desire and the discipline to work at it. Michael Gelb, in his book; HOW TO THINK LIKE LEONARDO DA VINCI, suggests that we:

- Keep a journal
- Jot down ideas, impressions and observations as they occur.
- In your notebook, make a list of 100 questions that you think are important.
- Review your list and choose the 10 that seem most significant.
- Rank the ten in order of importance to you.
- Set aside a time to contemplate the first question on your list.
- Explore the alternatives, look for themes and relationships, concentrate, until you are satisfied that you have a valid answer.
- Repeat with each question.

Develop an insatiable curiosity. The continuous quest for learning is a powerful force.

One of the ultimate purposes of life is to learn. Learning gives life meaning and helps us understand life's meaning. Learning enables more effective decision making.

Deliberately expose yourself to new experiences, ideas, information and opinions. Consciously and continuously strive to be more aware, more knowledgeable and more understanding of everything that is relevant to you. Learning can be fun, not a chore, if you *decide* it is fun. Life will be more interesting and exciting if you are constantly learning.

"Never try to be better than anyone else, but never cease to be the best you can be."

Coach John Wooden

Your life is shaped largely by the decisions you make. The more skills you develop, (like problem solving skills, human relations skills, etc.) and the more knowledge you acquire (about things like: how the world works, why people act the way they do, etc.), the better your decisions will be, and the better the quality of your life will be.

Learn from experience. Doing the same thing over and over and expecting different results is one of the definitions of insanity. Doing *more* of what doesn't work, does not work. Focus on what does work and do more of that. When traditional solutions don't work, create new approaches to try.

The world and life are constantly changing. To cope, to thrive, we must adapt. To remain adaptive, we must be committed to a life of continuous learning.

"The capacity to learn is a *gift.*
The ability to learn is a *skill*.
The willingness to learn is a *choice"*

Brian Herbert

2. <u>Learn to Listen.</u>

Many important decisions involve other people. The most useful skill to learn for dealing effectively with people is the skill of listening, really LISTENING. Real listening can't happen unless you have a sincere desire to understand what you're hearing, and that's not an easy task to manage. Real listening requires intention, concentration and effort. Listening may seem like giving up power because you are not in control of the conversation. In fact, it enhances the probability of effective outcomes. "When you stop preaching and really listen, here's what happens": (from THE 7 HABITS OF HIGHLY EFFECTIVE PEOPLE, by Stephen Covey)

- **People are more willing to trust you**. If you don't have people's trust, you will never be able to influence them.
- **You acquire useful information**, which makes it much easier to find solutions.
- **You gain insight into other people's perceptions** and what it will take to make a solution acceptable to them.
- **You begin to see other people as individuals – and maybe even allies.** Together, you move from I/they to US.

168

- **You can develop solutions that other people are willing to accept and even support.** When people contribute to the solutions, become co-owners, they are more likely to commit and follow through.
- **When people feel heard, they are more willing to listen.** If people do not feel that you "get" them, they are not inclined to expend the effort to listen to and understand you.

This is not to say that listening guarantees a favorable outcome every time, but failure to listen usually guarantees that the outcome will not be optimal, and it may be a complete failure.

In THE 7 HABITS, Covey refers to this skill as "empathic listening", and urges us to "Seek First to Understand and then to be Understood".

He indicates that: "next to physical survival, the greatest need of a human being is to be understood, to be affirmed, to be validated, to be appreciated. Listening with empathy to another person provides that person with psychological 'air'. Once that need is met, you can move on to problem solving or influencing." If that need is not first met, the person will be too preoccupied with "gasping for air" to appreciate the wisdom of your solutions. He is not likely to listen to you until you have listened to him.

LEARN to listen. It's amazing what you will LEARN. LISTEN to learn, not to frame your reply.

3. Read.

"The more you read, the more things you will know. The more you know, the more places you'll go".

Dr. Suess

Experiences enhance your ability to make effective decisions. Seek out and take advantage of opportunities to create and embrace positive personal experiences. But there is a practical limit to what you can personally experience. There is a much broader scope of wisdom available, if you include learning from what others have written about experiences, whether fact or fiction, and what they learned from them.

"No matter how busy you think you are, you must find time for reading, or surrender yourself to self-chosen ignorance."

Atwood H. Townsend

Reading can take us to worlds we will never see and helps us understand and learn from people of cultures we will never encounter. It enables us to travel instantly through distance and time, to understand our origins, our heritage and the lessons of history. It helps us understand how the world works and why people act the way they do. It stretches our minds and helps us see the world in new ways. It increases our sensitivity to people and to nature. Reading changes lives. Reading can help us understand how to be better human beings.

"Employ your time in improving yourself by other men's writings so that you shall come easily by what others labored hard for."

Socrates

"Reading is everything. Reading makes me feel like I've accomplished something, learned something, become a better person. Reading makes me smarter.

Reading gives me something to talk about. Reading is escape, and the opposite of escape. It's a way to make contact with reality. It's a way of making contact with someone else's imagination. Reading is grist. Reading is bliss."

Nora Ephron

"What an astonishing thing a book is. It's a flat object made from a tree with flexible parts on which are imprinted lots of funny dark squiggles. But one glance at it and you're inside the mind of another person, maybe somebody dead for thousands of years. Across the millennia, an author is speaking clearly and silently inside your head, directly to you. Writing is perhaps the greatest of human inventions, binding together people who never knew each other, people of distant epochs. Books break the shackles of time. A book is proof that humans are capable of working magic."

Carl Sagan

4. Use Time Wisely

Time is limited. Be conscious of it. Make the most of it. This is not to imply that you should work all the time. Everyone needs to spend time having fun, learning, exercising, spiritually recharging and just relaxing. Just be conscious of the importance of time and intentional about how you use it.

5. Control What You Say When You Talk to Yourself.

We all talk to ourselves constantly. Make the tone of those conversations positive, not critical or negative. Don't beat yourself up for mistakes or shortcomings. Don't delude yourself about reality but focus on accomplishments and successes. Understand your feelings but focus on your behavior. You feel the way you feel because of what you do. If you want to change how you feel, change what you are doing. Anger and fear are major impediments to rational decision making. Talk with yourself about your anger and fears. Ask yourself how you would like to act if you were not angry or afraid.

"You can't go back and change the beginning, but you can start where you are and change the ending."

Anonymous

6. Think Before You Speak

Both Buddhist and Muslim wisdom teachers advise that, before we speak, we should pass what we intend to say before three gatekeepers, in the form of these three questions:

Is what we are about to say true?
Is what we are about to say necessary?
Will what we are about to say do no harm?

7. Be Adaptive.

We are constantly making decisions, big and small. These choices are about who we are, what we should change, and how. Our challenge is to make the changes positive and productive.

"Be the change that you wish to see in the world."

Mahatma Gandhi

We are all involved in many roles: friend, spouse, parent, sibling, son, daughter, student, employee, supervisor, group member, etc. etc. Striving to become better at fulfilling those roles is a worthwhile objective. It enriches our lives and the lives of others. Becoming stagnant or failing to fulfil our responsibilities in these roles means falling short of our potential and losing touch with current reality.

If you want your life to be more fulfilling, you must change mindset and behavior. Resisting change is self-limiting. It shuts off possibilities and opportunities.

> "The world as we have created it is a result of our thinking. It cannot be changed without changing our thinking."

> Albert Einstein

Our focus should be on how to make changes that make us, our relationships and the world better, not worse. Resolving and striving to become better persons and to help improve the lives of others, are worthwhile goals, and increase the probability that inevitable changes will be positive.

> "The only way that we can live, is if we grow. The only way that we can grow is if we change. The only way that we can change is if we learn. The only way we can learn is if we are exposed. And the only way that we can become exposed is if we throw ourselves out into the open. Do it. Throw yourself."

> C. JoyBell

Change for the sake of change is a waste. Change for improvement is invaluable. Improvement will not happen without change.

"For what it's worth: it's never too late or, too early to be whoever you want to be. There's no time limit, stop whenever you want. You can change or stay the same. There are no rules to this thing. We can make the best or the worst of it. I hope you make the best of it. And I hope you see things that startle you. I hope you feel things you never felt before. I hope you meet people with a different point of view. I hope you live a life you're proud of. If you find that you're not, I hope you have the courage to start all over again."

Eric Roth,

CHANGE – don't fight it. Adapt to it. Promote it!

"Incredible change happens in your life when you decide to take control of what you do have power over, instead of craving control over what you don't."

Steve Maraboli,

8. Be Persistent.

Not all of your choices will turn out to be good ones. YOU WILL FAIL! (That's a good thing). It's not just OK, it's essential.

"I do not think that there is any other quality so essential to success of any kind as the quality of perseverance. It overcomes almost everything."

John D. Rockefeller

Those who excel at whatever they do have learned to learn from failures. The excellent fail more often than the mediocre. They begin more. They attempt more. They succeed because they have failed more and learned from their failures.

It is only from the experience of challenging ourselves that we learn and grow, and we often mature and learn more from our failures than from our successes. When we put ourselves on the line, when we fall down and get up again, we become stronger and more resilient.

You will fail. It will never be particularly pleasant. The key is to learn from the process. Consciously reflect on the process and ask: "what did I learn that will be of benefit for my next decision?"

Failure does not have to be an end point. If a goal is worthy, if an approach did not work and if you learned from the experience, trying again with a modified approach is a viable option.

"PRESS ON
Nothing in the world can take the place of persistence.
Talent will not; nothing is more common than
unsuccessful people with talent.

Genius will not; unrewarded genius is almost a proverb.
Education alone will not; the world is full of educated
derelicts.
Persistence and determination alone are omnipotent."
Anonymous

I have had this quote on my wall for years and found its truth apparent in multiple instances.

"A failure is not always a mistake. It may simply be the

best one can do under the circumstances. The real mistake is to stop trying"

B. F. Skinner

"Through perseverance many people win success out of what seemed destined to be certain failure."

Benjamin Disraeli

How much you can learn when you fail determines how far you will go in achieving your goals.

D. APPRECIATE LIFE

1. Choose to Think

People who live meaningful, effective and fulfilling lives think differently than those who don't. To accomplish anything, you have to take action, and the success of the action depends on the thoughts that initiated it. All that one achieves or fails to achieve is the direct result of one's thoughts.

Think about who you are. Think about who you want to be. Think about what you love. Think about what is sacred. Think about what is true. Think about what you want to learn. Think about your values and principles. Think about the fact that you will die and that this day is a gift. Think about what is important. Think about what is priceless. Think about how you wish to live your life.

Be a "critical" (not negative but questioning) thinker. Ask: What evidence, experience, authority supports this statement, contention, theory? Is the evidence verifiable and complete? Are the premises valid? Are my intentions honorable, and right for all concerned?

176

Effective thinking is seeking the whole picture, looking for relationships, looking for patterns rather than pieces. To make effective decisions about how to live, it is critical to develop the ability to reason accurately and independently, rather than accepting answers based upon authority or tradition.

Clear thinking involves effectively gathering, accessing and integrating the multiple messages coming at us from the reality around us and within us. The characteristic that makes us uniquely human is the ability of our minds to examine their own processes, to think about thinking. We can, and should, mentally examine: How did I reach that conclusion? Was my conclusion influenced by my prejudices? Is my conclusion logical or does it reflect the way I want things to be? What are my goals and objectives? Will this decision enable or impede my goals? What kind of person do I want to be? Are my actions consistent with who I want to be?

Thinking clearly takes commitment, effort and practice. The benefits are well worth the effort. Our ability to think, and to think about thinking, is a tremendous gift. We use it or lose it.

2. Choose to Make Your Life Meaningful

Seek the wisdom to do the right thing. Wisdom is about more than thinking. It is choosing to live wisely, aligning actions with valid principles.

Life is an endless quest, a search for wisdom and for experiences that enlighten. Finding meaning and purpose takes effort, introspection and wise choices about principles and values. It means being open to direction from a Higher Intelligence, searching inside for the real you. It involves deciding what kind of person one chooses to be and what kind of life one wants to live.

> "The value of life lies not in the length of days, but in the use we make of them; a man may live long yet live very little."

Michel Eyquem de Montaigne

In the end, meaning is very personal. We each have a responsibility to determine a purpose for our lives that has significance for us. At least a part of that task is to develop ourselves into the most wise, moral, strong and loving persons we can be and to live in peace with a clear conscience. At the same time, we must understand that a "good" life is a quest and a process, not a state of being. We cannot be perfect.

> "We are visitors on this planet. We are here for ninety, a hundred years at the very most. During that time we must try to do something good, something useful with our lives. Try to be at peace with yourself and help others share that peace. If you contribute to other people's happiness, you will find the true goal, the meaning of life."

The Dalai Lama

3. Choose to Let Your Life Speak

The real you is not revealed by what you believe or what you profess, but by what you do. Let the way you live your life demonstrate who you are. Doing good enables you to be good and to feel good.

Commit to truth.

Practice Integrity.

Live ethically and morally.

Serve others.

Search for understanding and wisdom.

Keep first things first.

Treat people with kindness and compassion.

Support justice & fairness for all.

4. Choose to Really Live

Make a decision to make better decisions. Making better decisions will improve the quality of your life. One of the most important, fundamental, decisions that you can make is to decide to live your life fully, not just take up time and space, but really live.

Imagine you only have ten hours to live. What would you do?

Imagine you only have ten days to live. What would you do?

Imagine you only have ten months to live. What would you do?

Contemplate your answers to these questions. What would you do differently if you knew the exact amount of time you had left? How would you redesign/refocus your life? Assuming that you would do something differently, why should not knowing the duration of your life keep you from starting that redesign now, from changing your focus now?

"None of us know how much time we have to live, but we know it is finite. However long or short it is, we should live it to maximize: the joy of family and friends, service to others, and making the most of our potential. *"It's only when we truly know and understand that we have a limited time on earth – and that we have no way of knowing when our time is up – that we will begin to live each day to the fullest, as if it was the only one we had."*

Elizabeth Kübler-Ross

Develop a bias for action. Live life, don't just let it happen. DO SOMETHING to:

- Ease the burdens of others.
- Help others grow and realize their potential.
- Mold your character to align with valid principles.
- Demonstrate kindness
- Learn, grow and realize your personal potential.
- Teach someone something useful
- Promote social justice.
- Improve relationships between people.
- Preserve the beauty of nature.

One of my favorite observations about life was written by George Bernard Shaw:

"Life is no brief candle to me. It is a sort of splendid torch which I have got a hold of for the moment, and I want to make it burn as brightly as possible before handing it on to future generations. I want to be thoroughly used up when I die, for the harder I work, the more I live. I rejoice in life for its own sake. This is the true joy of life: being used for a purpose recognized by yourself as a worthy one, being thoroughly worn out before being thrown on the scrap heap, being a force of nature instead of a selfish little clod of ailments and

grievances complaining that the world will not devote itself to making you happy."

Every day, do something to make you a better you. Every day, learn something new. Every day, demonstrate compassion for someone. Strive to live the kind of life for which Saint Francis of Assisi prayed:

"Lord make me an instrument of your peace.

Where there is hatred let me sow love.

Where there is injury let me sow pardon.

Where there is doubt, faith.

Where there is despair, hope.

Where there is darkness, light.

And where there is sadness, joy."

Life is precious! CHOOSE TO REALLY LIVE IT.

APPENDIX A

DEFINING YOUR VALUES

1. The following is a list of 75 common personal values cited by persons asked about such things. Add to the list any other that you believe important to you, and combine any two or more that you consider similar enough to be considered as one.

Accountability	Accuracy	Status
Tenacity	Self Confidence	Commitment to Family
Achievement	Goodness	Fun
Wealth	Gratitude	Financial Security
Compassion	Ambition	Integrity
Balance/Harmony	Work Ethic	Leisure
Calmness	Assertiveness	Physical Safety
Commitment	Belonging	Independence
Freedom	Control	Happiness
Dependability	Cooperation	Contentment
Fairness	Spirituality	Physical Fitness
Friendship	Creativity	Personal Growth
Faith	Health	Serenity
Generosity	Serving Others	Thoughtfulness
Respect	Stability	Structure
Competitiveness	Challenge	Logic
Consistency	Love	Reliability
Excitement	Dependability	Being Organized
Fame	Persistence	Learning/Education
Contribution	Intelligence	Inclusiveness / Diversity
Courtesy	Respect For Nature	Artistic Expression
Creativity	Humility	Empathy
Decisiveness	Self-Control	Justice
Determination	Being Responsible	Loyalty
Expertise	Success	Truth Seeking

2. From your modified list, check or circle the 12-15 you consider most important.

3. For each of the 12-15 selected, write down a definition of what the term means to you. Writing the definitions forces you to really think about what the concepts mean and why they are important. The following are examples of such definitions:

- Honesty & Integrity – To be honest is to be real, genuine, authentic, to deal equitably with others, to not take things to which you have no right and to always tell the truth.
- Responsibility – Responsible people are those who take charge of themselves and their conduct. Ultimately, we are responsible for the kinds of persons we have made of ourselves. Being responsible means meeting commitments and being accountable for our actions.
- Work Ethic – Work is expending energy for the sake of accomplishing something or achieving something. It is doing something worthwhile that one can take pride in doing well. Work should be viewed as something positive, something of value, not punishment or drudgery. The opposite of work is not play or having fun, but idleness, not investing ourselves in anything, wasting time.

4. From that list of 12-15, select the 7 that are most important to you and rank them in order of priority from one to seven. To facilitate the ranking process, imagine that you have 100 points to invest in these values. Allocate points to each of the values until you are satisfied with the ranking. The point spread will provide an indication of the relative importance of the values to you.

It may also be useful to approach the ranking by considering the values in "pairs", i.e. evaluate two values and determine which of the two is more important. Continue the process until there is a clear #1. Then continue the process until you identify #2, etc., etc.,

An Example

Rank	Value	Definition	Value Points
1	Goodness	Being a "good" person, living a "good" life, means thinking and acting in ways consistent with one's core values.	19
2	Love	Love should be viewed as a verb, an active something we do. Love means sharing pain and celebrating pleasures. Love means caring, respecting, encouraging, wishing another well and helping when possible.	18
3	Integrity/Honesty	To be honest is to be real, genuine, authentic, to deal equitably with others, to abstain from taking things to which we have no right and to always tell the truth	14
4	Commitment to Family	Committing to family means making family a priority, always being there to provide support when needed, making time for family, enjoying family, creating and sustaining family traditions, strengthening and nurturing family relationships.	14
5	Compassion/ Empathy	Compassion is different than pity. Empathy involves seeing oneself in another's place, to attempt to understand. Practicing compassion is feeling another's pain and being motivated to help relieve it. Sharing and buffering suffering is one of our highest callings. We are all in this together.	12
6	Justice	Justice is about being fair, equitable. It derives from the principle that all persons have certain "unalienable rights" and the principle of "moral rightness", the concept that there are basic moral and ethical standards that determine how people should be treated. Is this solution fair to all concerned?	12
7	Learning/Education/ Personal Growth	Learning gives life meaning and helps us understand life's meaning. The more skills we develop (like problem solving skills, human relations skills, etc.), and the more knowledge we acquire (like about: how things work, why people act the way they do, etc.), the better our decisions will be, and thus, the better the quality of our lives will be	11
		Total Points	100

YOUR VALUES WORKSHEET

Rank	Value	Definition	Value Points
1			
2			
3			
4			
5			
6			
7			
		Total Points	100

1. Confirm your values. (review and evaluate).
   - Would acting in accordance with these values make you feel good about yourself?
   - Are these really your values or values that someone told you that you should have?
   - Would you be proud to share these values with someone you admire and respect?
   - Would you be willing to stick with and defend these values in situations where others might disagree with or attack them?

2. Make a copy of your VALUES WORKSHEET. Keep this short list in your wallet or purse.

3. When deliberating about a decision, test your short list of choices against this list to determine how consistent each option is with your core values.

A SELF PERCEPTION CHECKLIST

Circle a number from 1 to 7 indicating your belief about how true the statement is about you.
7 = Strongly Agree. 1 = Strongly Disagree.

Statement	1	2	3	4	5	6	7
1. Others can depend on me.	1	2	3	4	5	6	7
2. I am intelligent.	1	2	3	4	5	6	7
3. I care about other people.	1	2	3	4	5	6	7
4. I exercise self control.	1	2	3	4	5	6	7
5. I use my time wisely.	1	2	3	4	5	6	7
6. I am a good friend.	1	2	3	4	5	6	7
7. My friends significantly influence what I think and do.	1	2	3	4	5	6	7
8. I am happy for others when they do well.	1	2	3	4	5	6	7
9. I'm a good listener.	1	2	3	4	5	6	7
10. I keep my commitments.	1	2	3	4	5	6	7
11. I am well organized.	1	2	3	4	5	6	7
12. I am almost always on time.	1	2	3	4	5	6	7
13. I set goals & objectives.	1	2	3	4	5	6	7
14. I enjoy working in a team.	1	2	3	4	5	6	7
15. I like to learn.	1	2	3	4	5	6	7
16. I am proud of things I have accomplished.	1	2	3	4	5	6	7
17. I enjoy learning from people who are different than me.	1	2	3	4	5	6	7
18. I am interested in a wide variety of things.	1	2	3	4	5	6	7
19. I tend to be more positive than negative.	1	2	3	4	5	6	7
20. I get upset by significant changes.	1	2	3	4	5	6	7
21. I don't have many friends.	1	2	3	4	5	6	7
22. I am kind to other people.	1	2	3	4	5	6	7
23. I like myself.	1	2	3	4	5	6	7
24. I accept responsibility for what I say and do.	1	2	3	4	5	6	7
25. I am a good member of my family.	1	2	3	4	5	6	7
26. I enjoy helping others.	1	2	3	4	5	6	7
27. I care a lot about what others think of me.	1	2	3	4	5	6	7
28. It bugs me when people of authority tell me what to do.	1	2	3	4	5	6	7
29. I appreciate and try to protect nature.	1	2	3	4	5	6	7
30. My life has meaning.	1	2	3	4	5	6	7

Be honest. This exercise is for you. Think carefully about your answers. Are there any characteristics you would like to change?

APPENDIX C

A SELF PERCEPTION CHECKLIST		Date:						
Circle a number from 1 to 7 indicating your belief about how true the statement is about you. 7 = Strongly Agree. 1 = Strongly Disagree.								
1. Others can depend on me.	1	2	3	4	5	6	7
2. I am intelligent.	1	2	3	4	5	6	7
3. I care about other people.	1	2	3	4	5	6	7
4. I exercise self control.	1	2	3	4	5	6	7
5. I use my time wisely.	1	2	3	4	5	6	7
6. I am a good friend.	1	2	3	4	5	6	7
7. My friends significantly influence what I think and do.	1	2	3	4	5	6	7
8. I am happy for others when they do well.	1	2	3	4	5	6	7
9. I'm a good listener.	1	2	3	4	5	6	7
10. I keep my commitments.	1	2	3	4	5	6	7
11. I am well organized.	1	2	3	4	5	6	7
12. I am almost always on time.	1	2	3	4	5	6	7
13. I set goals & objectives.	1	2	3	4	5	6	7
14. I enjoy working in a team.	1	2	3	4	5	6	7
15. I like to learn.	1	2	3	4	5	6	7
16. I am proud of things I have accomplished.	1	2	3	4	5	6	7
17. I enjoy learning from people who are different than me.	1	2	3	4	5	6	7
18. I am interested in a wide variety of things.	1	2	3	4	5	6	7
19. I tend to be more positive than negative.	1	2	3	4	5	6	7
20. I get upset by significant changes.	1	2	3	4	5	6	7
21. I don't have many friends.	1	2	3	4	5	6	7
22. I am kind to other people.	1	2	3	4	5	6	7
23. I like myself.	1	2	3	4	5	6	7
24. I accept responsibility for what I say and do.	1	2	3	4	5	6	7
25. I am a good member of my family.	1	2	3	4	5	6	7
26. I enjoy helping others.	1	2	3	4	5	6	7
27. I care a lot about what others think of me.	1	2	3	4	5	6	7
28. It bugs me when people of authority tell me what to do.	1	2	3	4	5	6	7
29. I appreciate and try to protect nature.	1	2	3	4	5	6	7
30. My life has meaning.	1	2	3	4	5	6	7
Be honest. This exercise is for you. Think carefully about your answers. Are there any characteristics you would like to change?								

APPENDIX D

In the spaces below, list some of the things you can do to demonstrate acceptance of those who may "appear" to be different from you.

1. _____

2. _____

3. _____

4. _____

5. _____

6. _____

7. _____

APPENDIX E

COMMUNICATING WITH FRIENDS

Because he/she is your friend, your friend may be particularly sensitive to things that you say and do, and/or significantly influenced by what you say or do (i.e. copy what you say or do). List below some of the things that you should never say or do to a friend.

1. NEVER INFLUENCE A FRIEND TO PARTAKE OF POTENTIALLY DANGEROUS DRUGS!

2. _____

3. _____

4. _____

5. _____

6. _____

7. _____

8. _____

9. _____

10. _____

11. _____

APPENDIX F

GOALS WORKSHEET

Date _____

Goals are statements (decisions) about what you want to accomplish and stand for in your life. They should include statements about the kind of person you want to be, what you want to accomplish, and what you want to experience. Goals are long term and general. Goals should reflect your values and establish the direction and parameters of your life.

#1 _____

_____

_____

#2 _____

_____

_____

#3 _____

_____

_____

#4 _____

_____

_____

#5 _____

_____

_____

#6 _____

_____

_____

#7 _____

_____

_____

#8 _____

_____

_____

APPENDIX G

OBJECTIVES WORKSHEET

Date _____

Objectives define results that are to be accomplished, stated in very specific, measurable terms, within a specified time. Objectives are the building blocks for the attainment of Goals.

1 _____

_____

_____

2 _____

_____

_____

3 _____

_____

_____

4 _____

_____

_____

5 _____

_____

_____

6 _____

_____

_____

#7 _____

_____

_____

8 _____

_____

APPENDIX H

OPPORTUNITIES TO GIVE BACK

1. Visit someone in a nursing home
2. Volunteer at your local animal shelter
3. Organize a Park cleanup with friends.
4. Help with yard work for elderly or unwell neighbors
5. Volunteer at a local soup kitchen
6. Become a mentor to a young person
7. Volunteer at an After School program
8. Donate your hair to charities like Wigs for Kids or Children With Hair Loss
9. Donate blood at the Red Cross
10. Collect and donate gently used coats and sweatshirts to a local charity
11. Teach English as a second language as a literacy volunteer
12. Tutor students
13. Volunteer to help build homes with Habitat for Humanity.
14. Register to become an organ donor
15. Volunteer at an equine therapy center
16. Coach a local youth team
17. Volunteer at Meals on Wheels
18. Volunteer at a Hospital
19. Recycle
20. Volunteer at a Wilderness Center
21. Volunteer to read to kids at the local library, nursery or preschool
22. Collect food to donate to food pantries
23. Volunteer at a local non-profit agency. Check with the United Way for suggestions and contacts
24. Organize a fund-raising event for a local charity
25. Volunteer with an Adaptive Sports Program
26. _____
27. _____
28. _____
29. _____
30. _____

The activity to which I commit to become involved within the next two weeks:

_____

Date: _____

APPENDIX I

OTHERS WHO WOULD BE AFFECTED BY MY ADDICTION

Drug use is not just about you. Others would inevitably be affected. In the spaces below list the names of those who could be affected, if you became addicted or a "user".

1. _____

2. _____

3. _____

4. _____

5. _____

6. _____

7. _____

8. _____

9. _____

10. _____

11. _____

12. _____

13. _____

14. _____

15. _____

APPENDIX J

A PERSONAL PLEDGE TO MYSELF

I understand that marijuana, nicotine and alcohol, like the illegal drugs, are all mind and body altering substances and potential killers.

I understand that my use of these substances can have harmful effects on me, my family, my friends and total strangers.

I CHOOSE to maintain personal control over my mind and body.

I THEREFORE PLEDGE THAT:

_____ I will never use illegal drugs.

_____ I will never use marijuana.

_____ I will never use products containing nicotine.

_____ I will never drink alcoholic beverages.

OR

_____ If I drink alcoholic beverages, I will limit my consumption to one drink per day.

X _____ (Signature)

Date _____

FRAMING WORKSHEET
Why is a Decision Required? What are the Root Causes of the Issue?
What is the Real Issue?

How Important is the Issue?   Comments

	1	Paramount	
	2	Significant	
	3	Material	
	4	Mundane	

What Are the Real Needs?

What Are My Objectives?

Primary:

Secondary:

What Are the Real Constraints?

What Are My Relevant Personal Preferences?

By When Should the Decision Be Made?

Required Date   _____

Target Date   _____

Comments

APPENDIX L

CONSEQUENCES WORKSHEET				

Description of the Issue _____
_____
_____

Alternative #	1	2	3	4
Alternative Description				
Likely Positive Outcomes				
Probability				
Likely Negative Outcomes				
Probability				
Values Reinforced				
Goals/Objectives Supported				

196

IMPACT WORKSHEET				
Description of the Issue				
Alternative #	1	2	3	4
Alternative Description				
Person/Group Impacted				
Likely Positive Impacts				
Likely Negative Impacts				

APPENDIX N

IMPLEMENTATION PLAN WORKSHEET				
ACTION	By Whom	By When	Tools/Resources Required	Who To Involve

POST MORTEMS - EVALUATING PAST DECISIONS
Date _____

Issue as Defined: _____

Targeted Outcome: _____

Actual Outcome: _____

Reasons for Differences _____

What did I learn about, what would I do differently about, the following?

Framing the Issue _____

Gathering information _____

Identifying Alternatives _____

Considering Consequenses _____

Impact on Others _____

Thinking it Through _____

If I were making the decision today, I would: _____

APPENDIX P

MORE DECISION-MAKING TECHNIQUES

Morphological Analysis.

Fritz Zwicky, an astrophysicist who is credited with the discovery of what is referred to as dark matter, developed a process for systematically expanding the number of viable options to be considered when attempting to resolve a problem or issue. The process has been labeled "Morphological Analysis" or "Zwicky's Box." The steps of the process are as follows:

1. Carefully define/frame the issue.
2. Identify the relevant elements/parameters of the issue.
3. List the parameters across the top axis of a grid.
4. Under each parameter, list viable options for that parameter.
5. Hold one option of one parameter constant and consider combining it with each of the options in the other columns. Some combinations will be ridiculous, some untenable, but some may represent ideas with potential.
6. Discard those combinations that are impossible or unworkable. Add the viable ones to your list of alternatives for analysis.

Consider the following illustration:

Issue - Develop a new toy to add to the company product line.

	PARAMETERS					
	Theme	Target Age Group	Material	Color	Gender	Price Range
OPTIONS						
	Space	3 to 5	Plastic	Red	Male	$5 to $10
	Action	6 to 9	Wood	Blue	Female	$11 to $15
	Animal	10 to 12	Metal	Green	Both	$16 to $20
	Sports			Pink		$21 to $30
	Cars			Yellow		
	Party					

Figure P-1

The highlighted combination: an action toy for boys ages 10 to 12 made from blue plastic, priced in the $16 to $20 range, is one of several hundred that could be considered using the model. Looking at the various possible combinations may lead to concepts that would never have been considered otherwise.

200

Matched Pairs

Another simple, but somewhat subjective method is to rank alternatives by conducting "matched pair comparisons":

List the alternatives in any order.

> Alternative 1
> Alternative 2
> Alternative 3
> Alternative 4
> Alternative 5

Compare alternatives 1 and 2. If 2 appears more effective than 1, move it ahead of 1. The list now looks like this:

> Alternative 2
> Alternative 1
> Alternative 3
> Alternative 4
> Alternative 5

Repeat the process. Compare 3 to 1. If 3 looks better than 1, move it ahead of 1.

Compare 3 to 2. If 3 is better move 3 to the top of the list.

Continue the process until you have arranged the list in your perceived order of effectiveness. You may end up with a list that looks entirely different from the original:

> Alternative 3
> Alternative 2
> Alternative 1
> Alternative 5
> Alternative 4

Estimate & Adjust From a Reference Point

A very useful tool for making decisions that involve some sort of measurement, and for which precise data is impossible or difficult to obtain, is sometimes referred to as the "estimate and adjust" technique. We select a value that is "easy" to determine or estimate and make judgements about how much to adjust from that point. In real estate it is common to estimate the market value of a property by analyzing the actual selling prices of similar properties, calculating an average, then making a judgement about whether the subject property is better or worse than average, and "how much" better or worse.

To lend credibility to a decision, we attempt to start with a "known" value and adjust from there. The base becomes a "reference point".

This technique is useful when the reference point is reasonably accurate. It will serve us well much of the time.

However, as Dr. Ryan Hamilton, Professor at Emory University's Business School, observes: "The idea of reference points is that almost every evaluation we make is not made in absolute terms but, rather is relative to something else. Interestingly, these reference points are quite fluid and contextual - even arbitrary. We are so dependent on reference points that when we don't have good ones, we are often willing to use unimportant, erroneous, or even irrelevant reference points to make decisions."

Reference points matter. We even use them to evaluate personal performance. A study by psychologists Scott Meday, Victoria Medvec and Thomas Gilovich indicated that in sporting events, bronze medalists were often happier than silver medalists. Each competitor's happiness, level of satisfaction, was determined by the reference point chosen.

- For silver medalists, the natural reference point is first place, the gold medal. They came so close to being the "best". They are disappointed to come in "second".
- For the bronze medalist, the reference point is fourth place, getting no medal and no recognition at all. They are delighted to be one of the "winners".

Reference points can be useful in situations where agreement between parties is necessary. They are valuable decision making tools when used intelligently and can save valuable time. First, assure that you are <u>aware</u> that you are utilizing reference points in your decision-making process and then carefully analyze the validity of the points used. When disagreements arise in dealing with others, examine the situation to determine if differences in reference points could be cause of conflicts. It is easier to craft win/win solutions if you understand the reasons for disagreements.

SHORTCUTS

Everyone uses shortcuts in decision making. Used prudently, they can be effective for saving valuable time and mental energy. None guarantee a correct decision every time, but some will yield satisfactory results most of the time. Their use can also cause serious problems when employed as a substitute for thorough analysis and sound judgement. As with other tools and processes described in this text, it is imperative to match the process and mental effort with the importance of the decision.

The fifty-cent word for shortcuts, as used in decision theory, is "heuristics". A heuristic is a way of simplifying a complex process or situation, often by relating the unknowns in a situation to something known, or easier to "know", than the real issue. Heuristics are typically used in decisions involving the assessment of the probability of uncertain events occurring (e. g. predicting the winner of an upcoming baseball world series) or the value of uncertain quantities (e. g. predicting the average rate of inflation over the next three years). Heuristics are not decision rules, but process shortcuts that are often used for assessing probabilities and predicting values.

Noted psychologists Amos Tversky and Daniel Kahneman conducted extensive research regarding the use of heuristics in decision making under conditions of uncertainty. The following is a brief summary of some of their published findings and conclusions about commonly used heuristics:

Anchoring and Adjustment. This heuristic is used often when estimating numerical values or orders of magnitude. You start with a number you know and adjust from there, based upon your perception of how different the specific case is from the chosen base point. In estimating the height of a particular basketball player, you might start with the understanding that the average male is 5' 10" tall and estimate how much taller this fellow is than average, perhaps when he is standing next to an average size referee.

While this shortcut can be useful, recognize that the validity of the process is dependent upon two key elements: selecting an appropriate anchor point and estimating an appropriate degree of adjustment. Mistakes with the first can have particularly adverse consequences. Different starting points can lead to significantly different estimates. Research has shown that exposure to a number, even an irrelevant number, during the process of formulating a problem can influence the choice of the anchor point. In one Tversky and Kahneman clinical trial, the median estimate of the number of African countries in the United Nations was 25 for a group exposed to the number 10 during preliminary discussions. For a similar group exposed to the number 65 during preliminary discussions, the median estimate was 45. Our minds can play tricks on us and latch on to irrelevant associations. Pay attention to selecting the anchor and be sure it makes sense.

Research has also indicated a significant tendency to underestimate the sufficiency of the mental adjustment. Typically, people's estimates stick too close to the anchor point. Think through the adjustment.

Representativeness. This kind of shortcut is sometimes used to categorize something or someone as belonging to a class on the basis of observing characteristics representative of the class.

This kind of shortcut can be very useful. Doctors use it every day to diagnose medical causes from observations and descriptions of symptoms. They infer that the problem here must be influenza, because the symptoms are similar to those in thousands of cases of influenza observed before. They tend to be right most of the time.

This kind of heuristic can be disastrous, however, if used as the basis for stereotyping (as it often is). To use an example from the news, it can be totally erroneous to assume that because someone is a Muslim, that person must be a terrorist, when in fact less than .001% of the Muslims in the world belong to or support any kind of terrorist organization or activity.

Jumping to conclusions based upon unfounded generalizations about race, gender, religion or national origin is an unwise use of the representativeness heuristic.

This is not to say that you should avoid mental shortcuts. The key to using any of these heuristics effectively is to: be aware that you are doing so, consciously determine that this is what you want to do, carefully determine that the heuristic fits the issue, and avoid the cognitive errors to which they can sometimes lead.

APPENDIX Q

SOME CONSIDERATIONS AND CAUTIONS OF WHICH YOU SHOULD BE AWARE

A. Tradeoffs & Compromises – Dealing With Conflicting Objectives

It is unusual for a significant decision to involve only a single objective. Most often, prudently making an important decision requires that we consider multiple objectives, some of which may conflict, or even be mutually exclusive. These issues cannot be resolved by focusing on just one objective. One alternative may be superior on some objectives but inferior on others. When faced with such situations, you have to make choices, which can sometimes be challenging.

Objectives that involve cost and/or time are types that often require tradeoffs. It is common for cost and quality to conflict, and for the ideal solution to lie somewhere beyond a time constraint.

When there are multiple decision criteria (objectives) and some conflict, using the Weighted Score technique can help evaluate alternatives. When weights and scores are equal, they cancel each other out and other objectives become the deciding factors. An effective model allows for objectives of equal weights and alternatives with equal scores for some criteria. It helps bring into focus the overall picture.

In situations where most criteria are judged to be roughly equal, scoring just the most critical may be of value.

Assume that in the college selection process you establish as one objective to attend the college with the highest academic rating that will accept you, and a second objective to avoid exceeding a certain education related debt limit upon graduation. You are accepted at schools A, B & C. School A has an academic rating 10% higher than B, costs 20% more than B and would require that you exceed your debt limit. School C has the lowest academic rating (just slightly lower than B), and also the lowest cost. Something has to give.

CRITERIA	Weight	College A		College B		College C	
		Raw Score	Wghted Score	Raw Score	Wghted Score	Raw Score	Wghted Score
Academic Rating	10	100	1,000	90	900	80	800
Cost/Debt	7	80	560	90	630	100	700
Total Wghted Score			1,560		1,530		1,500

Figure Q-1

If all other criteria are judged to be roughly equal, College B looks like a reasonable choice. Note that a key decision here is the relative weights given to academics and cost.

Be sure that all important criteria are included in the analysis.

Assume that you are considering a job change. You have interviewed for two new jobs. You have an offer for Job A and the company representative indicates that they want your decision by the end of the week. Your evaluation of the jobs indicate that job A is acceptable, but you rate Job B higher than Job A and Job B pays 5% more than Job A. However, the company representative for Job B indicates that they will not be making a decision for at least two weeks. You believe that the probability that you will receive the Job B offer is about 60%. You understand that, because of a pending retirement, there will be an opportunity opening up in your department in about four months. That job would pay about 10% more than your present salary. You access your chances of getting that job at about 40%. Do you take the "sure thing", hold out for the possibility of the "better" job offer or stay put and bet on the promotion?

A Point to Ponder: What are some criteria other than pay that should be considered in reaching a decision?

Eliminate Alternatives. When faced with multiple alternatives and conflicting objectives, you may be able to simplify the process by eliminating one or more alternatives, by comparing your evaluations of how each fulfills your objectives. If option C is better than B and A on a major objective and no worse on your other objectives, B and A can be eliminated. If a clear winner does not emerge by employing this process, you can at least make the choice easier by narrowing the field.

B. LOGIC TRAPS

Most choices are made under conditions of uncertainty. While some shortcuts or heuristics can be helpful and save valuable time, others can lead you astray. What appear initially to be perfectly logical conclusions can turn out to be totally irrational and detrimental. In the interest of simplifying issues and saving time, our minds can play tricks on us. We need to be cautious of these "logic traps", which reflect how our minds tend to work, but which can lead to faulty decisions. Some of these traps are the result of personal biases; some are the result of fuzzy thinking. The best way to guard against these flaws in thinking is to be aware that they exist and to learn to recognize, and make adjustments, when they are affecting your decision-making process.

The following is a summary of some of the common logic traps and a brief description of how they can impair sound decision making:

Sunk Costs. One of the most common of these logical errors is the result of what scientists have labeled the "sunk cost bias". People have trouble admitting they were wrong when a decision does not turn out well. They may rationalize or ignore the mistake and then make another poor decision in an attempt to "rescue" or justify the first.

The management team of a corporation was faced with a decision about investing $1,000,000 in a project involving the launch of a new product. They had already spent $5,000,000 on the project and so far, it was not doing well. The project was over budget and, to date, results in the marketplace were disappointing. One of the arguments advanced by proponents was that "we have already spent $5,000,000; therefore, we should risk another $1,000,000 to protect the $5,000,000". They spent the additional $1,000,000. The product failed. The project was abandoned. The team had poured good money after bad, because of a reluctance to acknowledge a $5,000,000 mistake.

The team failed to acknowledge that the $5,000,000 was a "sunk cost". It was irretrievable. The $1,000,000 additional investment should have been viewed entirely on its merits: what will we get for the $1,000,000? The $5,000,000 was rationally irrelevant to the $1,000,000 decision.

This same reluctance affects personal decisions. When faced with a decision about making a major expenditure to repair an auto, many will be more likely to opt for the expenditure, rather than junking the auto, if they had recently spent a significant amount for other repairs to the same auto;

the rationale being that they would lose the cost of the previous repair if they decide not to make the current one. Rationally, the cost/benefit of the current expenditure should be viewed independently. The expense of the previous repair is a sunk cost.

Avoid inappropriately allowing unalterable and irrelevant past events to influence decisions about the future:

Two young fans are debating whether or not they should attend their favorite football team's Sunday game. The weather is terrible. It is alternatively raining and snowing. Winds are gusting 20 to 30 mph. The forecast is for more of the same. It is sure to be very uncomfortable in the stands. One is arguing for opting out of attendance, saying that it makes no sense to risk their health in the inclement weather and that they will be physically miserable. The other argues that they have already purchased their expensive tickets and would be "wasting" that money if they don't attend.

Rationally, the fact that they had paid for tickets should not affect the decision. The expenditure for the tickets is a "sunk cost". It is gone. The money spent for the tickets is the same whether "A", they choose to go to the game, or "B", they choose not to go. <u>Whenever a consequence is the same for every alternative, it is not relevant to choosing an alternative.</u>

Stating the Issue Correctly. Don't treat the definition of a decision issue casually. How an issue/problem is defined has a significant impact on the assessment and selection of choices. Psychological studies indicate that when two objectively equivalent questions are posed in different ways, choices can vary dramatically. A study published by Tversky and Kahneman illustrates this point. The question posed and the resulting preferences were as follows:

> "Imagine that the US is preparing for the outbreak of an unusual Asian disease, which is expected to kill 600 people. Two alternative programs to combat the disease have been proposed. Assume that the scientific estimates of the consequences of the programs are as follows:
>
> - If Program A is adopted, 2000 people will be saved. (alt selected by 72%)
> - If Program B is adopted, there is a 1/3 probability that 6000 people will be saved, and a 2/3 probability that no people will be saved (alt selected by 28%)

Which of the two programs would you favor?

When the question was rephrased to reflect lives lost rather than lives saved, the preferences were almost opposite.

- If Program C is adopted, 4000 people will die. (alt selected by 22%)
- If Program D is adopted, there is a 1/3 probability that nobody will die, and a 2/3 probability that 6000 people will die. (alt selected by 78%)

(Tversky and Kahneman, "The Framing of Decisions and the Psychology of Choice")

Note that all four alternatives yield exactly the same expected result – 2000 lives saved yet changing the frame of reference in the issue statement significantly changed the choices of the decision makers.

Give a great deal of attention to how you define a decision issue. Don't accept the first definition. Recast it in different words. State it as positively as reasonable and restate it as negatively as is reasonable. Refine it until you are satisfied that it truly reflects the issue to be resolved. It matters.

Deviation from the Mean. Many mistakenly view chance as a self-correcting process. Having witnessed five tosses of a coin come up heads, they are willing to bet that the next toss will come up tails, because a tails result is "due". They know that the odds are 50-50 for either heads or tails. They assume that a deviation in one direction will induce a deviation in the other direction, to balance the long-term odds. In fact, the probability of a heads result on the sixth toss is still 50%. You need to understand and rationally apply probabilities.

Wishful Thinking. When assessing possible outcomes, people tend to overestimate the probability of desirable outcomes and underestimate the probability of undesirable results. Clearly identify what you want to have happen and rationally assess if that is influencing what you are predicting will happen. Describe the circumstances to one or more persons whose judgements you trust, without disclosing your predictions, and see how closely their assessments of probable outcomes match yours.

Denial. Similarly, when discovering information that is inconsistent with their wants, some tend to deny that information, often by attempting to discredit the source. You should evaluate sources and objectively weigh all evidence.

Slanting Estimates. Many decisions require estimates of future events or conditions. Some people are conservative, some are optimistic. Using estimates that are too conservative or too optimistic can have serious consequences.

Assume that you are in charge of production planning for a company that produces complex, high priced widgets with long production times. Based upon your experience, you believe that the number of widgets your company can sell next year depends upon:

1. The growth rate of the national economy.
2. The growth rate of your particular industry.
3. Your company's market share.

In the current year, total industry shipments of the type of widgets your company produces are projected to be 10,000 units. Your company expects to ship 2,000 units for a 20% market share. You seek expert advice about what to expect next year.

You consult an economist whose published projection is for a 2.5% growth in the economy. He really expects 3% but does not want a reputation for being optimistic. In his world the pain for estimating low is much less than the pain for estimating high.

You consult an industry expert who estimates that based upon a 2.5% growth in the economy (he consulted the same economist that you did), he expects industry unit sales to grow by 4% next year. He really expects 6% growth but chooses to be cautious.

You consult your company's VP of Sales and he tells you that he thinks he can increase your company's market share to 21%. He really thinks the share will be 22% because of some new product features. (His bonus is tied to how much he beats his own sales forecast).

	Production Plan Based upon <u>official</u> source estimates	Production Plan Based upon "<u>real</u>" source estimates
Economy Growth	2.5%	3.0%
Industry Growth	6.0%	4.0%
Industry Units	10,400	10,600
Market Share	21%	22%
Company Units	2,184	2,332
Difference in Units Projected		148

Figure Q-2

If these widgets sell for $150,000 each, the difference in dollar sales is 148 X 150,000 = $22,200,000. If the company earns a 40% gross profit on the widgets, the potential profit impact is $8,880,000, not exactly pocket change. If, based on the best information available, you tell the CEO that the company should gear up to build 2,184 units next year, the company may forego nearly $9 million in additional profit, all because your estimators choose to be just a little bit prudent, cautious, conservative in their estimates.

The same is true for optimism. If you use estimates that are just a little bit optimistic, the cumulative effect could result in millions of dollars of unsold inventory at the end of the year, and you out of a job.

Unlike this contrived example, most of your decisions will not have $9 Mil implications. The point here is that even presumably small increments in estimates can have major implications. Choose only reliable sources. Check multiple sources and reconcile differences. Conduct sensitivity analyses of estimates over a range of values to assess the impact of each on the final decision. Double check key numbers. Be as objective as possible. Resist the temptation to be conservative or optimistic.

This is not an exhaustive list of the possible "logic traps" that can cloud decision making. The purpose is to alert you to these types of potential problems. The key to avoiding these, and other traps, is awareness and careful analysis. Think it through!

BIBLIOGRAPHY

Armstrong, Karen. *TWELVE STEPS TO A COMPASSIONATE LIFE.* New York, NY. Anchor Books. 2010.

Aronson, Brad. *HUMAN KIND, Changing the World One Small Act At a Time.* Los Angeles, CA. LifeTree Media. 2020.

Bevelin, Peter. *SEEKING WISDOM, From Darwin To Munger.* Malmo, Sweden. Post Scriptum, AB. 2003.

Branden, Nathaniel. *THE ART OF LIVING CONSCIOUSLY, The Power of Awareness to Transform Everyday Life.* New York, NY. Simon & Shuster. 1997.

........*TAKING RESPONSIBILITY, Self Reliance and the Accountable Life.* New York, NY. Simon & Shuster. 1996.

Clarke, Cyril. *DETERMINED: Young People in the Middle.* Bloomington IN. iUniverse Books. 2013

Covey, Sean. *THE 7 HABITS OF HIGHLY EFFECTIVE TEENS.* New York, NY. Fireside – Simon & Shuster. 1998.

-----------------. *THE 6 MOST IMPORTANT DECISIONS YOU'LL EVER MAKE.* New York, NY. Fireside – Simon & Shuster. 2006.

Covey, Stephen R. *THE 7 HABITS OF HIGHLY EFFECTIVE PEOPLE.* New York, NY. Simon and Shuster. 1989.

De Bono, Edward. *SERIOUS CREATIVITY.* London, England. Harper Collins Business. 1992.

Diamandis, Peter M. Steven Kotler. *ABUNDANCE, The Future is Better Than You Think.* New York, NY. Free Press. 2012.

Dickson, Douglas N., Ed. *USING LOGICAL TECHNIQUES FOR MAKING BETTER DECISIONS.* New York, NY. John Wiley & Sons, Inc. 1983.

Divine, Mark. *UNBEATABLE MIND.* Mark Divine. 2015.

Fox, Mark L. *DA VINCI AND THE 40 ANSWERS, A Playbook for Creativity and Fresh Ideas.* Austin, TX. Wizard Academy Press. 2008.

Garrett, Michael. *WALKING ON THE WIND, Cherokee Teachings for Harmony and Balance.* Rochester, VT. Bear & Company, Publishers. 1998.

Gelb, Michael J. *HOW TO THINK LIKE LEONARDO da VINCI..* New York, NY. Delacorte Press. 1998.

Hammond, John S., Keeney, Ralph L., Raiffa, Howard. *SMART CHOICES, A Practical Guide To Making Better Decisions.* Boston Mass. Harvard Business School Press. 1999.

Hanh, Thich Nhat. *THE MIRACLE OF MINDFULNESS, A Manual on Meditation.* Boston, MA. Beacon Press. 1976.

Hill, Percy H. et al. *MAKING DECISIONS, A Multidisciplainary Introduction.* Lanham, MD. University Press of America, Inc. 1986.

Johnson, Spencer, MD. *YES or NO, The Guide to Better Decisions.* New York, NY HarperCollins Publishers, Inc. 1992.

Juniper, Dean. *MAKING DECISIONS, How to Develop the Skills That Make For Good Decisions.* Oxford, United Kingdom. How To Books. 1998.

Keyes, Ken Jr. *TAMING YOUR MIND, A Guide To Sound Decisions.* Coos Bay, Oregon. Love Line Books. 1975.

Leman, Dr. Kevin. *SMART KIDS, STUPID CHOICES.* Ventura, CA. Regal Books. 1982.

Lindner, Ken. *CRUNCH TIME, 8 Steps to Making the Right Life Decisions at the Right Times.* New York, NY. Penguin Group (USA) Inc. 2005.

Mandino, Og. *A BETTER WAY TO LIVE.* New York, NY. Bantam Books. 1990.

-------------------. *THE CHOICE.* New York, NY. Bantam Books. 1984.

Matlock, Mark. *WISDOM ON MAKING GOOD DECISIONS.* Grand Rapids, MI. Zondervan. 2008.

McGervey, John D. *PROBABILITIES IN EVERYDAY LIFE.* New York, NY. Ballantine Books. 1989

Minirth, Frank B., MD and Paul D. Meier, MD. *HAPPINESS IS A CHOICE.* Grand Rapids, MI. Baker Book House. 1978.

Muller, Wayne. *HOW THEN SHALL WE LIVE?* New York, NY. Bantam Books. 1996.

Nerburn, Kent ed. *THE WISDOM of the NATIVE AMERICANS.* New York, NY. MJF Books. 1999.

Newman, Susan. *YOU CAN SAY NO TO A DRINK OR A DRUG.* New York, NY. The Putnam Publishing Group. 1986.

----------------------. *IT WON"T HAPPEN TO ME.* New York, NY. The Putnam Publishing Group. 1987.

Pokras, Sandy. *SYSTEMATIC PROBLEM SOLVING AND DECISION MAKING.* Casto Valley, CA. The Viability Group. 1989.

Rath, Tom. *LIFE'S GREAT QUESTION.* Jackson, TN. Silicon Guild Books. 2020

Reichert, Richard. *MAKING MORAL DECISIONS, Living our Christian Faith.* Winona, MN. St. Mary's College Press. 1979.

Schultz, Ron. *UNCONVENTIONAL WISDOM, Twelve Remarkable Innovators Tell How Intuition Can Revolutionize Decision Making..* New York, NY. Harper Collins Publishers, Inc. 1994

Shinabarger, Jeff. *YES or NO, How Your Everyday Decisions will Forever Shape Your Life.* Colorado Springs, CO. David C. Cook. 2014.

Shore, Bill. *THE CATHEDRAL WITHIN.* New York, NY. Random House. 1999.

Smedes, Lewis B. *CHOICES, Making Right Decisions in a Complex World.* San Francisco. Harper & Row. 1986.

Stutz, Phil, Barry Michels. *THE TOOLS.* New York, NY. Spiegel & Grau. 2012.

Welch, David A. *DECISIONS, DECISIONS, The Art Of Effective Decision Making.* Amherst, NY. Prometheus Books. 2002.

Wilson, Paul F., Larry D. Dell, Gaylord F. Anderson. *ROOT CAUSE ANALYSIS.* Milwaukee, WI. ASQ Quality Press. 1993.

Wooden, John, Don Yaeger. *A GAME PLAN FOR LIFE.* New York, NY. Bloomsbury USA. 2009.

--------------------, Steve Jamison. *WOODEN, A Lifetime of Observations and Reflections On and Off the Court.* Lincolnwood, IL. Contemporary Books. 1997.

Woodward, Orrin. *RESOLVED, 13 Resolutions for Life.* Cary, NC. Obstacles Press. 2018.

Zane, Edoardo Binda. <u>EFFECTIVE DECISION-MAKING,</u> *How to Make Better Decisions Under Uncertainty and Pressure.* Edoardo Binda Zane. 2016.